THINKING ABOUT LOGIC

THINKING ABOUT LOGIC

Classic Essays

EDITED BY

Steven M. Cahn
City University of New York Graduate Center

Robert B. Talisse
Vanderbilt University

Scott F. Aikin
Vanderbilt University

WESTVIEW PRESS

A MEMBER OF THE PERSEUS BOOKS GROUP

Library of Congress Cataloging-in-Publication Data
Thinking about logic : classic essays / edited by Steven M. Cahn, Robert B. Talisse. Scott F. Aikin.
     p. cm.
  ISBN 978-0-8133-4469-0 (alk. paper)
  1. Logic. I. Cahn, Steven M. II. Talisse, Robert B. III. Aikin, Scott F.
  BC6.T45 2011
  160—dc22
                            2010017146

10 9 8 7 6 5 4 3 2 1

CONTENTS

III. LOGIC AND INFERENCE

IV. LOGIC AND FREEDOM

V. LOGIC AND REALITY

PREFACE

The study of logic raises philosophical questions about knowledge, meaning, rationality, and reality. Most textbooks in the field, however, pass by such matters in order to focus exclusively on principles of formal reasoning and strategies of formal proof. The assumption appears to be that discussion of the larger philosophical themes would be a distraction from the mastery of technique. Yet one can find a number of short, gripping, accessible essays that display the subject's wider significance.

This reader contains fifteen of these classic articles in the philosophy of logic. The collection is usable with any logic textbook and can bring additional perspective to any logic course. The selections have been chosen for their brevity, clarity, and impact. They deepen understanding of fundamental concepts of logic, while displaying connections between logic and other areas of philosophy, including metaphysics, epistemology, philosophy of science, and philosophy of language.

We wish to take this opportunity to thank our editor, Karl Yambert, for his firm support and wise counsel. We also appreciate the kind assistance of the staff at Westview Press.

I

LOGIC
AND
KNOWLEDGE

If you deduce from two propositions, p and q, a third, r, then presumably you first need to believe s, that p and q imply r. You then also need to believe t, that p, q, and s imply r. And so on. Thus it seems that any inference requires an infinite number of steps.

To reason correctly from premises to conclusion, we need rules of inference. Are they themselves further premises? If so, Lewis Carroll's story of Achilles and the Tortoise demonstrates the inherent regress that develops. W. J. Rees suggests that the apparent regress is a consequence of confusing premises with meta-premises for inference. J. F. Thomson argues that agreeing to rules for inference is implicit in committing to any premise, and so the rules themselves should not be treated as additional premises.

1

What the Tortoise Said to Achilles

Lewis Carroll

Achilles had overtaken the Tortoise, and had seated himself comfortably on its back.

"So you've got to the end of our race-course?" said the Tortoise. "Even though it *does* consist of an infinite series of distances? I thought some wiseacre or other had proved that the thing couldn't be done?"

"It *can* be done," said Achilles. "It *has* been done! *Solvitur ambulando.* You see the distances were constantly *diminishing;* and so—"

"But if they had been constantly *increasing?*" the Tortoise interrupted. "How then?"

"Then I shouldn't be *here,*" Achilles modestly replied; "and *you* would have got several times round the world, by this time!"

"You flatter me—*flatten,* I mean," said the Tortoise; "for you *are* a heavy weight, and *no* mistake! Well now, would you like to hear of a race-course, that most people fancy they can get to the end of in two or three steps, while it *really* consists of an infinite number of distances, each one longer than the previous one?"

"Very much indeed!" said the Grecian warrior, as he drew from his helmet (few Grecian warriors possessed *pockets* in those days) an enormous note-book and a pencil. "Proceed! And speak *slowly,* please! *Shorthand* isn't invented yet!"

"That beautiful First Proposition of Euclid!" the Tortoise murmured dreamily. "You admire Euclid?"

"Passionately! So far, at least, as one *can* admire a treatise that wo'n't be published for some centuries to come!"

"Well, now, let's take a little bit of the argument in that First Proposition—just *two* steps, and the conclusion drawn from them. Kindly enter them in your note-book. And in order to refer to them conveniently, let's call them *A*, *B*, and *Z*:—

(*A*)   Things that are equal to the same are equal to each other.

(*B*)   The two sides of this Triangle are things that are equal to the same.

(*Z*)   The two sides of this Triangle are equal to each other.

Readers of Euclid will grant, I suppose, that *Z* follows logically from *A* and *B*, so that any one who accepts *A* and *B* as true, *must* accept *Z* as true?"

"Undoubtedly! The youngest child in a High School—as soon as High Schools are invented, which will not be till some two thousand years later—will grant *that*."

"And if some reader had not yet accepted *A* and *B* as true, he might still accept the *sequence* as a *valid* one, I suppose?"

"No doubt such a reader might exist. He might say 'I accept as true the Hypothetical Proposition that, *if A* and *B* be true, *Z* must be true; but, I *don't* accept *A* and *B* as true.' Such a reader would do wisely in abandoning Euclid, and taking to football."

"And might there not *also* be some reader who would say 'I accept *A* and *B* as true, but I *don't* accept the Hypothetical'?"

"Certainly there might. *He*, also, had better take to football."

"And *neither* of these readers," the Tortoise continued, "is *as yet* under any logical necessity to accept *Z* as true?"

"Quite so," Achilles assented.

"Well, now, I want you to consider *me* as a reader of the *second* kind, and to force me, logically, to accept *Z* as true."

"A tortoise playing football would be—" Achilles was beginning

"—an anomaly, of course," the Tortoise hastily interrupted. "Don't wander from the point. Let's have *Z* first, and football afterwards!"

"I'm to force you to accept *Z*, am I?" Achilles said musingly. "And your present position is that you accept *A* and *B*, but you *don't* accept the Hypothetical—"

"Let's call it *C*," said the Tortoise.

"—but you *don't* accept

(*C*)   If *A* and *B* are true, *Z* must be true."

"That is my present position," said the Tortoise.

"Then I must ask you to accept *C*."

"I'll do so," said the Tortoise, "as soon as you've entered it in that note-book of yours. What else have you got in it?"

"Only a few memoranda," said Achilles, nervously fluttering the leaves: "a few memoranda of—of the battles in which I have distinguished myself!"

"Plenty of blank leaves, I see!" the Tortoise cheerily remarked. "We shall need them *all*!" (Achilles shuddered.) "Now write as I dictate:—

(*A*)   Things that are equal to the same are equal to each other.

(*B*)   The two sides of this Triangle are things that are equal to the same.

(*C*)   If *A* and *B* are true, *Z* must be true.

(*Z*)   The two sides of this Triangle are equal to each other."

"You should call it *D*, not *Z*," said Achilles. "It comes *next* to the other three. If you accept *A* and *B* and *C*, you *must* accept *Z*."

"And why *must* I?"

"Because it follows *logically* from them. If *A* and *B* and *C* are true, *Z must* be true. You don't dispute *that*, I imagine?"

"If *A* and *B* and *C* are true, *Z must* be true," the Tortoise thoughtfully repeated. "That's *another* Hypothetical, isn't it? And, if I failed to see its truth, I might accept *A* and *B* and *C,* and *still* not accept *Z,* mightn't I?"

"You might," the candid hero admitted; "though such obtuseness would certainly be phenomenal. Still, the event is *possible*. So I must ask you to grant *one* more Hypothetical."

"Very good. I'm quite willing to grant it, as soon as you've written it down. We will call it

(*D*)   If *A* and *B* and *C* are true, *Z* must be true.

Have you entered that in your note-book?"

"I *have*!" Achilles joyfully exclaimed, as he ran the pencil into its sheath. "And at last we've got to the end of this ideal race-course! Now that you accept *A* and *B* and *C* and *D*, *of course* you accept *Z*."

"Do I?" said the Tortoise innocently. "Let's make that quite clear. I accept *A* and *B* and *C* and *D*. Suppose I *still* refused to accept *Z*?"

"Then Logic would take you by the throat, and *force* you to do it!" Achilles triumphantly replied. "Logic would tell you 'You ca'n't help yourself. Now that you've accepted *A* and *B* and *C* and *D*, you *must* accept *Z*!' So you've no choice, you see."

"Whatever *Logic* is good enough to tell me is worth *writing down*," said the Tortoise. "So enter it in your book, please. We will call it

(*E*)   If *A* and *B* and *C* and *D* are true, *Z* must be true.

Until I've granted *that*, of course I needn't grant *Z*. So it's quite a *necessary* step, you see?"

"I see," said Achilles; and there was a touch of sadness in his tone.

Here the narrator, having pressing business at the Bank, was obliged to leave the happy pair, and did not again pass the spot until some months afterwards. When he did so, Achilles was still seated on the back of the much-enduring Tortoise, and was writing in his note-book, which appeared to be nearly full. The Tortoise was saying "Have you got that last step written down? Unless I've lost count, that makes a thousand and one. There are several millions more to come. And *would* you mind, as a personal favour, considering what a lot of instruction this colloquy of ours will provide for the Logicians of the Nineteenth Century—*would* you mind adopting a pun that my cousin the Mock-Turtle will then make, and allowing yourself to be re-named *Taught-Us*?"

"As you please!" replied the weary warrior, in the hollow tones of despair, as he buried his face in his hands. "Provided that *you*, for *your* part, will adopt a pun the Mock-Turtle never made, and allow yourself to be re-named *A Kill-Ease*!"

What Achilles Said to the Tortoise

W. J. Rees

*(Being a revised account of a famous interview,
first reported in* Mind *in April, 1895, by Lewis Carroll.)*

Achilles, as is well known, had overtaken the Tortoise, and had seated himself comfortably on its back, thus proving that he *could* overtake the Tortoise, although the race-course consisted of an infinite series of distances.

Whereupon the Tortoise turned mathematician once more and presented Achilles with a most perplexing problem in logic.

"Would you like to hear," he said, "of a race-course that most people fancy they can get to the end of in two or three steps, while it *really* consists of an infinite number of distances, each one longer than the previous one?"

"Very much, indeed!" said the Grecian warrior, as he drew from his helmet an enormous note-book and a pencil. "Proceed! And speak *slowly,* please! *Short-hand* isn't invented yet!"

"That beautiful First Proposition of Euclid!" the Tortoise murmured dreamily. "You admire Euclid?"

"Passionately! So far, at least, as one *can* admire a treatise that won't be published for some centuries to come!"

"Well, now, let's take a little bit of the argument in that First Proposition—just *two* steps, and the conclusion drawn from them. Kindly enter them in your note-book. And in order to refer to them conveniently, let's call them A, B, and Z:

(A)   Things that are equal to the same are equal to each other.

(B)   The two sides of this triangle are things that are equal to the same.

Therefore

(Z)   the two sides of this triangle are equal to each other.

Readers of Euclid will grant, I suppose, that Z follows logically from A and B, so that anyone who accepts A and B as true, *must* accept Z as true?"

"Undoubtedly! The youngest child in a High School—as soon as High Schools are invented, which will not be till some two thousand years later—will grant *that*."

"And if some reader had *not* yet accepted A and B as true, he might still accept the *sequence* as a *valid* one, I suppose?"

"No doubt such a reader might exist. He might say 'I accept as true the hypothetical proposition that, *if* A and B be true, Z is true; but, I *don't* accept A and B as true'. Such a reader would do wisely in abandoning Euclid, and taking to football."

"And might there not *also* be some reader who would say 'I accept A and B as true, but I *don't* accept the hypothetical'?"

"Certainly there might. *He,* also, had better take to football."

"And *neither* of these readers," the Tortoise continued, "is *as yet* under any logical necessity to accept Z as true?"

"Quite so," Achilles assented.

"Well, now, I want you to consider *me* as a reader of the *second* kind, and to present me with premisses which will enable me to deduce the truth of Z."

"You want me to present you with premisses which will enable you to deduce the truth of Z?" Achilles said musingly. "And your present position is that you accept A and B, but you *don't* accept the hypothetical—"

"Let's call it C," said the Tortoise.

"But you *don't* accept

(C)   If A and B are true, Z must be true."

"That is my present position," said the Tortoise.

"Then I must ask you to accept C."

"I'll do so," said the Tortoise, "as soon as you've entered it in that note-book of yours. Now write as I dictate:

(A)   Things that are equal to the same are equal to each other.

(B)   The two sides of this triangle are things that are equal to the same.

(C)   If A and B are true, Z must be true.

Therefore

(Z)   The two sides of this triangle are equal to each other."

"Now I see what you are driving at," said Achilles. "You want me to say that if one accepts A and B and C as true, then one *must* accept Z as true?"

"Exactly! That's what I wanted you to say."

"And then," continued Achilles, "you are going to tell me that this is *another* hypothetical—we'll call it D—and that since you don't accept *this* hypothetical, you will still be able to accept A and B and C as true, but *not* Z?"

"Precisely!"

"And then, no doubt, you will ask me to enter *this* hypothetical again among my other premises, and say to you that, *if* you accept A and B and C and D as true, then you *must* accept Z as true?"

"I'll grant you; that *was* roughly what I expected."

"Well," said Achilles, "there's certainly a future for *this* kind of job! It will certainly go on until I shall have no more room in my note-book to write down the premises! Indeed, I should have to remain seated on your back for all time, trying to find sufficient premises to enable you to deduce the truth of Z!"

"Very true!" said the Tortoise triumphantly. "Very true, indeed! And now do you see that you have discovered what no logician is going to discover for centuries yet to come, an infinite regress?" (For the infinite regress had not yet *really* been invented). "And do you see," continued the Tortoise, "that no matter *how long* you try, you can never give me sufficient premises to enable me to deduce the truth of Z?"

"You do flatter me!" said Achilles. "I'll admit that I spotted the regress, but it was *you* who *invented* it."

"I *invented* it!" said the tortoise, with great astonishment. "One does not need to *invent* it; it is just *there,* and one can't do anything about it."

"No," said Achilles, "I'll stick to my point. *You yourself invented it.* You invented it by compelling me to write down that condition C with the other two conditions A and B, and so deceiving yourself into thinking that C was on the same footing as A and B. Did you want to deceive yourself, or were you just trying to tease *me?*"

"Neither, I assure you! But where else *could* you have inserted C? Can't you see that if my accepting the hypothetical is a *condition* of my accepting Z as true, it *must* be put in with the conditions A and B?"

"Well, yes and no. It must be put in with A and B but not on the same footing as A and B. By making C into an *extra* premiss you are substituting, as Aristotle might some day put it, a hypothetical argument for a syllogistic argument. Instead of saying 'A and B, therefore Z', you *now* say 'If A and B then Z, A and B, therefore Z'."

"Why!" said the Tortoise, "even an intermediate student can see *that*. But this only brings in *another* hypothetical. And since I don't accept *this* hypothetical, I can *still* accept all the premisses and deny the conclusion. You still haven't presented me with sufficient premisses to enable me to deduce Z."

"Not so fast!" replied Achilles, somewhat impatiently. "The trouble with *you* is that you don't see that there are hypotheticals *and* hypotheticals. You've never distinguished, have you, between first and second order hypotheticals?"

"When *I* did Honours," said the Tortoise, "there was certainly no news of them then."

"Well, then, I must briefly tell you about them. If I may use words which will only be understood in Oxford, and that only three thousand years hence, I would say that a second order hypothetical is a hypothetical which has another hypothetical—this time, a first order hypothetical—as its apodosis."

"Well, that *is* rather a mouthful! Could you not say it, please, in ordinary standard English—which is not yet invented, of course, but which will be appreciated in Oxford three thousand years from now?"

"By all means!" said Achilles, somewhat surprised to find so much humility and foresight all at once.

"A second order hypothetical," he continued, "states a condition under which *another* hypothetical is true. A hypothetical about a hypothetical! A *two-storeyed* hypothetical!"

"And, I suppose, this kind of hypothetical is important?"

"*Very* important! Can't you see that in a second order hypothetical the condition is always a condition on which we can make a true conditional statement, and not, therefore, a condition which can itself be included *in* that conditional statement?"

"I see *that* most clearly," said the Tortoise, "but what *has* this got to do with our argument?"

"This, surely: that the statement of the implication in a so-called hypothetical argument must generally take the form of a second order hypothetical, and *not* a first order hypothetical as would be the case with a syllogistic argument."

"Could you give an example? We *must* have examples, you know!"

"Well, let me see," said Achilles, "instead of saying that, if one accepts A and B and C one must accept Z, we must now say that, *if* one accepts C, *then*, if one accepts A and B, one must accept Z."

"Sounds a bit odd, doesn't it?"

"Not really. If A and B together imply Z, then, if both A and B are true, Z is true. Is there anything odd about that? If so, you can say instead that, if A and B are true, Z is true—provided A and B imply Z. And there's nothing odd about that! *That's* just ordinary standard English!"

"And I am to take it that this *has* got something to do with our argument?"

"Of course! You look at it like this: by making C an extra premiss *and at the same time* making the statement of the new implication a first order hypothetical, you have assumed that the hypothetical C can be included in its *own* protasis!"

"I have said, so to speak, that if A and B are true and that if it is true that if A and B are true Z is true, then Z is true?"

"That's right. And by making C an *indispensable* premiss you have further assumed that this hypothetical cannot be *true unless* it is included in its own protasis!"

"But in *that* case, . . ." said the Tortoise.

"In *that* case," said Achilles, "the hypothetical in the protasis must also be true and included in its own protasis, and so on, *ad infinitum.* Which means that C can never be true, although you have already accepted it as true!"

"The point, I suppose," said the Tortoise, "is that no hypothetical can be included in its *own* protasis. I'll take my stand with you on *that.* But what must I then say? Must I then say that C *cannot* be an extra premiss?"

"Not exactly. The trouble is that this word 'premiss' is a bit ambiguous. It may mean a proposition which, singly or jointly with others of the same order, implies a conclusion, or it may mean a proposition which implies that some *other* proposition or propositions of a different order imply a conclusion."

"For convenience," said the Tortoise, "let's call the first a *premiss,* and the second a *meta-premiss.* This is going to mean generally, of course, that the major premiss in what generations of logicians are going to call a hypothetical argument, will not be a premiss but a meta-premiss—but I suppose that is by the way."

"Quite so," said Achilles. "The point now is that C cannot be an extra *premiss,* but if by a premiss you mean a *meta-premiss,* then you can have C, if you like, as a premiss."

"Most confusing!" said the Tortoise. "Tell me this: you distinguish between the *premisses* of an inference and the *principle* of an inference?"

"Most certainly! No reader of Joseph and Russell—once they have written on the matter, of course—can object to *that* distinction."

"Very well then," said the Tortoise. "Are you now saying that the premiss of an inference is a first order statement, while the principle of an inference is a higher order statement, a statement about certain *other* statements, a meta-statement?"

"I am saying *that* much, certainly. We must distinguish between an argument, which is an *operation* with certain statements, and the principle of an argument, which is a *statement* about that operation."

"And, I suppose, the principle of an argument cannot *itself* be included among those *other* statements which are asserted *in* that argument? It cannot be *asserted,* in the way in which those *other* statements are asserted?"

"That is right. At least, not without destroying the argument, *or else* creating a new *kind* of argument."

"Such *delightful* sophistry!" murmured the Tortoise. "If I take to football, *you* will have to take to professional philosophy!"

"Is that a kind of *game*?" enquired Achilles.

"Of course," said the Tortoise. "It's a game in which everybody confuses everybody else, and the winner is the one who confuses most, and all the participants are Players and not Gentlemen."

"Then *I* will be a *Gentleman*," said Achilles.

"In that case," said the Tortoise, "you must give a straight answer. Are you, or are you not, saying that the *principle* of an inference cannot be an additional *premiss* of that inference?"

"I am saying *that*," said Achilles, "and more. The principle of an inference cannot be an extra premiss of the *same* inference. But *that* doesn't mean that it cannot be an extra premiss. What it *does* mean is that if you make it an extra premiss, then the inference becomes a different *kind* of inference, your new premiss will be a different *kind* of premiss, namely a meta-premiss, and the principle of this new inference will be a different *kind* of principle, namely one which can be stated only by means of a second order hypothetical."

"Good!" said the Tortoise. "I will now have C as a meta-premiss, and I will have the new implication statement as a second order hypothetical."

"Excellent!" said Achilles. "You are now on the right road. Proceed!"

"Suppose," continued the Tortoise, "I *reject* this second order hypothetical. Will you not then have to put it also among the premisses—sorry, meta-premisses—and so generate third, fourth, fifth order hypotheticals, and so on, *ad infinitum*? If so, you still haven't presented me with sufficient premisses, that is, meta-premisses, to enable me to deduce the truth of Z."

"Now, my dear Tortoise," said Achilles, "I must ask you to notice just one further point. A meta-premiss differs from a premiss in one important respect, that only *one* meta-premiss is ever necessary in any argument. For if one such meta-premiss is true, the premisses referred to *in* that meta-premiss are in fact *sufficient* to imply a conclusion. Any additional meta-premisses therefore are *quite* superfluous."

"Either C is *not* a premiss," said the Tortoise, recapitulating, "or if it *is* a premiss it is a meta-premiss, in which case *one* such premiss is sufficient in any argument. . . ."

"That is so," said Achilles, putting his note-book and his pencil back in his helmet—for *pockets* had not been invented in those days. "And I dare say," he continued, "that you will now find that you have sufficient premisses to enable you to deduce the truth of Z."

At this point the narrator, having some pressing business at the Bank, was obliged to leave. He overheard Achilles say, however, something or other about the off-side rule and the advisability of 'not handling the ball unless you are the goalkeeper'. The Tortoise replied that philosophy was 'nowadays a much better game than football'. On that most charming note the narrator drove off, and left the happy pair.

What Achilles Should Have Said to the Tortoise

J. F. Thomson

In 1895 Lewis Carroll published in *Mind*[1] a brief dialogue, 'What the Tortoise said to Achilles'. The intention of the story is, plainly enough, to raise a difficulty about the idea of valid arguments, a difficulty similar, or so Carroll implies, to Zeno's difficulty about getting to the end of a race-course. Different writers have said different things, usually briefly, about what the difficulty is. Let us first consider just what happens in the story and then try to see what problems it raises.

The topic of the story is a certain task set to Achilles. The Tortoise says that there might be someone who accepted the two propositions:

(A)   Things that are equal to the same are equal to each other, and

(B)   The two sides of this triangle are things that are equal to the same,

but did not accept

(C)   If things that are equal to the same are equal to each other, and if the two sides of this triangle are equal to the same, then the two sides of this triangle are equal to each other.

Such a person, he says, would not *as yet* (Lewis Carroll's italics) be under any logical necessity to accept the consequent of C, namely

(Z)   The two sides of this triangle are equal to each other.

He asks Achilles to pretend that he is such a person and to force him, 'logically', to accept Z. Since it is Achilles' failure to do this which is the point of the story, we must ask how his failure comes about.

Achilles sets about his task in an unexpected way. You might expect him to begin by trying to find out why the Tortoise does not accept C. Instead, he asks him to accept C, i.e. asks him to accept that very proposition which he has just said he does not accept. You might now expect the Tortoise to laugh, or to be surprised, or at least to say: 'But I don't accept C, or so we are pretending.' Instead he grants the request, or says he does, and for no other reason than that he has been asked to. He is now on record as having accepted A, B, and C. And now, Achilles says, he must accept Z. 'If you accept A and B and C, *you must* accept Z . . . because it follows *logically* from them.' The Tortoise replies in effect that just as there might be someone who did not accept the hypothetical C which connects A and B with Z so there might be someone who did not accept the hypothetical, call it D, which connects A and B and C with Z, and that such a person might accept each of A and B and C and still not accept Z. When Achilles asks him to accept D he does so, just as he accepted C, and the story goes on as before. Apparently the end of this 'ideal race-course' is never to be reached.

To see clearly what is happening, let us relabel the propositions involved. The original premises A and B we can collapse into one conjunctive premise C_0. The first hypothetical C we shall sometimes call 'C_1', the second, D, 'C_2', and so on. The hypothetical with antecedent X and consequent Y we shall call '$X \rightarrow Y$'. Then the sequence of propositions successively accepted by the Tortoise is

$$C_0 = (A \& B)$$
$$C_1 = C_0 \rightarrow Z$$
$$C_2 = (C_0 \& C_1) \rightarrow Z$$
$$C_3 = (C_0 \& C_1 \& C_2) \rightarrow Z$$

etc. The sequence is generated by the rule that the first term is (A & B) and each term thereafter is the hypothetical whose antecedent is the conjunction of the preceding terms and whose consequent is Z. The behaviour of the Tortoise also follows a simple inductive rule. He accepts the first term of the sequence. At each stage thereafter, having accepted C_0, C_1, . . ., C_n, he refuses to accept Z on the grounds that he has not yet accepted C_{n+1}, is asked to accept this one, does so, and the game goes on as before.

It is plain that as long as this procedure is adopted he will never be brought to accept Z. If at *every* stage Z is not to be accepted until some *other* proposition is accepted, Z will never be accepted. But the sensible reader will ask: 'So what?' Why should this procedure be adopted in the first place? How does, why should, an infinite sequence of hypotheticals C_1, C_2, . . . get into the picture?

The Tortoise represents himself as someone who accepts A and B but not C and he says that, being in this position, he is not *as yet* under any logical necessity to accept Z. This is wrong. Whether or not he accepts C, it is logically true. That means that the argument from A and B to Z is logically valid and that the Tortoise in accepting A and B commits himself to accepting Z. So he is already under a logical necessity to accept it. To say that he is not ('as yet') is precisely to deny that the argument 'A, B, ∴ Z' is logically valid. But if that were true there would be no problem; we should not expect Achilles to be able *logically* to force the Tortoise to accept Z on the basis of an invalid argument. It may be objected that the Tortoise is justified 'from his own point of view' in saying that he can accept A and B without accepting Z. The reply is that this point of view is a mistaken one and Achilles' task is precisely to make him give it up. How can he do that? He must first find out why the Tortoise does not accept C. Someone who was really unwilling or unable to grant the truth of this proposition would either have some reason, perverse or ingenious or both, for thinking it false or doubtful, or he would not have considered sufficiently carefully just what proposition it is. Perhaps there are other possibilities. But anyway Achilles must ask the Tortoise to show at least part of his hand. If the latter's pretence not to see that C is true is to be considered at all it must be taken seriously.

What Achilles does in the story is quite different. In effect he says: 'So you don't accept C. Well then, will you accept C?' To make such a request in such circumstances is ridiculous, and to accede to it is ridiculous too. Achilles makes it because, as he himself says, if you accept A and B and C you must accept Z—'it follows logically from them'. But this is a bad reason. In saying that Z follows from A and B *and C* Achilles implies that it does not follow from A and B alone, he implies that these premises are not by themselves sufficient. He thus accepts the implications of the 'not as yet' and so makes a nonsense of his acceptance of the idea that he should ('logically') force the Tortoise to accept Z. And anyway in so far as the latter is justified, 'from his own point of view', in not accepting Z, he would be justified also in refusing to accept C. He could say: 'Of course if I accept C I shall then have to accept Z, but that is not in question. You are trying to get me to accept Z. You can do that by presenting me with an argument which I see to be valid and which has premises which I am able to accept. I don't accept that the argument "A, B, $\therefore$ Z" is valid. So, as you should have foreseen, I can't accept C. So I can't accept all the premises of your second argument, "A, B, C, $\therefore$ Z". From the point of view of establishing its conclusion, a valid argument with false premises is no better off than an invalid one. In your case the falsity of the false premise in the second argument follows directly from the invalidity of the first. So not only does the second argument give me no more reason to accept Z than the first one did, but there is just the same lack of reason in each case.'

Given an argument with premises $P_1, P_2, \ldots P_K$ and conclusion Q let us call $(P_1, \& P_2 \& \ldots \& P_K) \rightarrow Q$ the hypothetical *associated with* that argument, and let us call the argument with the same conclusion and premises $P_1, P_2, \ldots, (P_1 \& \ldots \& P_K) \rightarrow Q$ the *strengthened form* of the original argument and a strengthened argument. An argument may fail to establish its conclusion on either or both of two counts; it may have one or more false premises, and, independently, the relation required to hold between the premises and the conclusion may not hold. It is clear that a strengthened argument will always be valid and so will never fail on the second count, and that if an argument fails on any count its strengthening must fail on the first of them. In particular, if an argument fails by not having enough premises its strengthening will escape that weakness but must, just because it is the strengthened form of that argument, fail by having an unacceptable premise. It follows that from the point of view of getting arguments which establish their conclusions the operation of strengthening is either redundant or futile.

We need not be inhibited from accepting this by feelings of loyalty to the old idea that some arguments have suppressed premises. Certainly, if the argument 'P, $\therefore$ Q' can have a suppressed premise, why should it not have the suppressed premise $P \rightarrow Q$? About the idea that arguments do have suppressed premises, a good deal needs to be said, but it does not need to be said here. For arguments which are said to have suppressed premises are said to be valid in virtue of having them, and valid arguments do not need to be strengthened. In other words, if we wish to say that an argument has suppressed premises we must take this seriously and really count the suppressed premises among its premises. (The observation that strengthening is either redundant or futile is quite independent of the question whether 'valid' must always mean 'logically valid' or whether logically valid arguments are just a subclass of valid arguments.)

All this, then, or part of it, is what the Tortoise could have said in reply to Achilles' request that he accept C. Instead, he accedes to the request and still does not accept Z. But is this inability the old inability in a new guise or is it a new one? Whether Lewis Carroll realized the fact or not, it is a new one. The failure to see the truth of C is, roughly speaking, a failure to appreciate the transitivity of the relation *sameness of length*. The failure to see that C_3 is true is a failure to appreciate the logical force of *if*. If there could be someone who thought that C_1 was false or doubtful, he might well be, and probably would be, someone who at once saw the truth of C_2. So at this second stage of the game the Tortoise has changed his ground. He began by representing himself as someone who could not accept a certain hypothetical. He now pretends to have accepted that hypothetical and represents himself as someone who does not see the truth of a quite different hypothetical. (And in a moment he will change his ground yet again; he will pretend to accept C_2 and will make difficulties over C_3. But these later subterfuges are not very interesting.)

We now see how the infinite sequence of hypothetical gets into the story. When he says that someone who accepts A and B but not C is not *as yet* under any necessity to accept Z, the Tortoise implies not only that the premises A and B are not sufficient but also that A and B and C would be, and also that he sees that this is so. When having accepted C he shifts his difficulty to C_2 he implies that if only he were able to accept that one he would be able to accept Z. So at each stage he introduces a new hypothetical into the discussion and tempts Achilles to ask him to accept it. The sequence of hypotheticals introduced in this way is infinite because however many premises he accepts he pretends not to see that there are enough.

We have also answered the question why Achilles fails in his task. His first mistake is in asking the Tortoise to accept C. By doing this he implies that he is not after all in any position to force him, logically, to accept Z. But if we think that his failure is a punishment for that mistake, we must be clear that the punishment does not fit the crime. For the Tortoise ought not to have acceded to the request and having acceded to it he ought to have accepted Z. So the second thing to be clear about is that the Tortoise cheats. Instead of presenting Achilles with just one problem he presents him with infinitely many; though this is concealed by the fact that Achilles does not really try to solve any of them.

The extreme eccentricity of the behaviour of both of the characters may well make us wonder whether Lewis Carroll knew what he was up to in writing the story. Certainly it cannot be merely taken for granted that he intended to advance some moderately clear thesis or theses about inference but chose to do so in a veiled and cryptic way. It is just as likely that the story is the expression of a perplexity by someone who was not able to make clear to himself just why he was perplexed. But we may still ask what points of logical interest emerge from it. I shall mention just two.

We say that if a triangle is isosceles the angles at the base must be equal, that if Tom is older than Dick and Dick older than Harry then Tom must be older than Harry. More generally we say that if such-and-such it must be the case that so-and-so. This use of 'must' is a signal that something is being claimed to follow from something else. But we also say: if you accept that such-and-such then you must accept that so-and-so. This use of 'must' can be misunderstood. 'I accept A and B and C and D', says the Tortoise at one point. 'Suppose I still refuse to accept Z?' 'Then Logic would take you by the throat and *force* you to do it', Achilles replies. But Logic does no such thing.

'If you accept the premises of a logically valid argument, you must accept its conclusion.' Well, *why* must he?—This statement does not mean that if someone does accept the premises of such an argument he will accept its conclusion, let alone that he will necessarily accept it. He may accept the premises without knowing or without noticing that they are the premises of a logically valid argument with that conclusion. Even when the argument is put before him he may be unable to understand it or unwilling to try. Or he may not see that it is valid, or may think that it contains such-and-such a fallacy. He may even say: 'Since the premises are true and the conclusion false the argument must be fallacious, though I can't for the moment see where the fallacy is.' Even when he has seen and examined the argument and convinced himself that it is valid he may still not accept the conclusion, since he may prefer to retract his acceptance of the premises. What is true is that in accepting the premises he *commits* himself to acceptance of the conclusion. Why? Because what we are here calling the conclusion is something that follows from premises which he accepts. But why then does acceptance of a set of premises commit one to acceptance of their consequences? This question can be regarded only as a request for an explanation of the notion of a consequence and of a logically valid argument or as an occasion to remind someone of what these notions are. Part of this explanation is that the set consisting of the premises of a logically valid argument and the negation of its conclusion is logically self-inconsistent and so must contain at least one falsehood. So anyone who accepts the premises and denies the conclusion has committed himself to at least one falsehood. This is the threat behind the 'must'. 'If you assert the premises and deny the conclusion, you will have said at least one false thing, however the facts may turn out to be.'

'If you accept these propositions you must accept that one'—this is characteristically said by someone who is trying to get his hearer to accept something. So it is said by someone who is or has been arguing. Then we may suppose that an argument has been put forward and that the hearer is or has been or soon will be examining it. But when the speaker says what he says he is only saying that the argument is valid. It follows that although this remark is typically made by someone who is arguing it is not itself a piece of an argument. It is one thing to put forward an argument, even a valid one, and another to say that you are arguing validly. It is one thing to propose for acceptance propositions which (you hope or believe or know) entail another proposition and another thing to say that they do. In arguing, you may need to point out that you are. You then (as it were) step aside from what you are doing and comment on your own performance. But then the performance must be there, independently of the comment, to be commented on.

The proposition that such-and-such an argument is valid can itself be a premise of an argument[2]. But it cannot be a premise in the argument to which it refers. If you want to say of some argument that it is valid you must be able to say what argument it is that you want to make this claim for. The argument must be identifiable. And the identification must be such as to allow the claim that it is logically valid to be assessed. To assess that claim we need to know what the premises are and what the conclusion is. So the premises must be identifiable independently of the claim that there are enough of them.

What has just been said about the statement that the argument '$P_1, \ldots, P_n, \therefore Q$' is logically valid must hold also of the statement that if P_1 and P_2 and . . . and P_n then necessarily Q. For the latter statement is logically equivalent to the former. It does not matter that the former argument is explicitly about an argument and the latter not. Just as the statement that an argument is logically valid cannot turn out to be a premise in that argument, so, and indeed very obviously, a hypothetical cannot turn out to be its own antecedent or a conjunct in its own antecedent. So if, having got you to accept premises P_1 to P_n and wanting you now to do what I think you are committed to doing, viz. accept Q, I assert that if P_1 and . . . and P_n then necessarily Q, I am not, or should not regard myself as, asking you to accept another premise. For *ex hypothesi* I suppose that you already have enough premises.

To say this is not to deny that some arguments have hypotheticals as premises and have them as premises in just the way they have other premises[3]. Someone who, having put forward some premises, puts forward a hypothetical having the conjunction of those premises as its antecedent may very well intend the hypothetical to be counted as another premise. If what is in question is the validity of your argument, it is up to you to say what its premises are. You may list as the set of premises enough to make it logically valid, and you may, either knowingly or unwittingly, list some that are redundant. All that is being said is that if you list your premises and all of your premises and then assert what we called the hypothetical associated with the argument whose premises these are, that hypothetical just cannot turn out to be one of the premises already listed. This rests on the fact that a hypothetical cannot be a conjunct in its own antecedent, and this rests in turn on the fact that no sentence which expresses a proposition can be longer than it is. It is therefore very obvious. But it is enough to clear up one of the misunderstandings in the story. When Achilles said that if you accept A and B and C you must accept Z he was claiming that the argument that since A, B, and C, therefore Z was logically valid, had *enough* premises, and so was not, or should not have regarded himself as, offering *another* premise.

So the first point of interest is that we must distinguish between arguing and talking about an argument, between giving reasons, even good ones, and saying that some reasons are good ones. In particular, if someone in arguing asserts a hypothetical and makes it clear, by using some such signal-word as 'must' or 'logically' or 'necessarily', that he regards it as necessarily true, he may be offering a premise and he may be doing something equivalent to commenting on a set of premises already identifiable. What he cannot be doing is both at once.

The second point is connected with the first. Before we can hope to understand what is going on between Achilles and the Tortoise we must be clear that to assert the truth (logical truth, or acceptability, or reasonableness, etc.) of a hypothetical is equivalent to asserting the validity (logical validity, or cogency, etc.) of the argument with which that hypothetical is associated. It follows that to accept the hypothetical is to commit oneself to accepting the validity of the argument. But what is it to accept the validity of an argument? One thing that shows that you accept it is that if you assert the premises you are willing to go on and say 'therefore' and then assert the conclusion. But then suppose that someone claims to accept the hypothetical and to accept the premise but is not willing to assert the conclusion? How can we get him actually to do what he is committed to doing, i.e. accept Q? It is natural to think of pointing out to him that Q follows logically from P and P→Q, and this thought may then seem suspect for something like the following reason: we began by wanting him to accept the argument 'P, ∴ Q' and now seem to be trying to get him to accept the (different) argument 'P, P→Q ∴ Q'; what if he will not accept this one either, shall we then have to start again? The suspicion is dispelled when we reflect that the latter argument really *is* different from the former one, so that someone might accept it and not accept the former. We must also remember that when we claim validity for the latter argument we are not, or at least should not regard ourselves as, arguing that since it is valid so is the original one. Such an argument would be fallacious. Strengthened arguments are always valid. So the second point of interest is that logically valid arguments are of different kinds. Consider for example the three arguments 'A, B, ∴ Z', 'A, B, C, ∴ Z' and 'B, ∴ Z'. The first is formalizable in first-order predicate logic with identity. The second is formalizable in truth-functional logic and in any one of a large number of weaker systems of propositional logic. The third, though logically valid, is not formally valid at all.

We naturally feel a reluctance to admit that someone could accept A, B and C and not accept Z. Behind this is the fact that if someone claims to accept the premises of a *very* simple argument and does not accept the conclusion it is sometimes reasonable to suppose that he has not really accepted the premises[4]. That is, we sometimes make it a necessary condition for someone's having accepted a set of propositions that he accepts such-and-such consequences of them. No general rules can be given for when this is reasonable, but it is probably a mere prejudice to think that the difficulty arises especially over 'A, B, C, ∴ Z' and does not arise at all over 'A, B, ∴ Z'. But the important point is that it is not the Tortoise's refusal to accept Z at the second stage that shows that Achilles was silly to offer him C as a premise at the first stage; even though Achilles was silly to do so, for reasons we have seen. What that refusal shows is rather something about the Tortoise.

In conclusion I should like to comment briefly on some remarks about the story in Professor G. Ryle's paper *If, So, and Because*[5]. Ryle is here considering the question: How does the validity of the argument 'P, ∴ Q' require the truth of the hypothetical P→Q? He discusses among others the following answer: 'The argument is always invalid unless the premise from which Q is drawn incorporates not only P but also P→Q. Q follows neither from P→Q by itself, nor from P by itself, but only from the conjunction P and (P→Q).' Ryle comments on this idea as follows: 'But this notoriously will not do. For, suppose it did. Then a critic might ask to be satisfied that Q was legitimately drawn

from P and (P→Q); and to be satisfied he would have to be assured that
if P and also if P and Q then Q. So this new hypothetical would have
to be incorporated as a third component of a conjunctive premise, and
so on for ever—as the Tortoise proved to Achilles. The principle of an
inference cannot be one of its premises or part of its premise. Conclusions are drawn from premises in accordance with principles, not from
premises which embody those principles.'

It seems that what Ryle calls the principle of an inference is either
what we have called the hypothetical associated with the argument or
some statement or formula of which that hypothetical is an exemplifi-
cation or a general proposition of which the hypothetical is a particular
case. In each of these cases his statement that the principle cannot be
one of the premises or part of its premise is clearly correct. It is hardly
necessary to repeat the argument: the 'principle' of the argument 'A,
B, ∴ Z' is, roughly speaking, the principle that a certain relation is tran-
sitive; if we strengthen that argument by adding the appropriate hypothetical as a redundant premise the new argument has a quite different
principle. But, more or less clearly implicit in what Ryle says, there is
the suggestion that Achilles fails in his task because he does not distinguish premises from principles, and, coupled with it, the idea that the
necessity for this distinction can be demonstrated by means of a
regress-argument. This does not seem correct.

We must notice first that the suggestion which Ryle is attacking is
much more seriously confused than his comment on it brings out. For
how in it are the letters 'P' and 'Q' being used? If they are constants
we can hardly be expected to assess the idea that the argument 'P, ∴ Q'
is not as it stands valid, since we have not been told what propositions
P and Q are. But if they are variables, the suggestion comes to this: no
argument is valid, but, given an argument, which will of course be invalid, we can always obtain from it an argument (its strengthened form)

which will be valid. And while it is absurd to hold that no arguments are valid, it is doubly absurd to hold this and then say that some arguments can be made valid. If for no values of 'P' and 'Q' does P yield Q, then, in particular, P & (P→Q) does not yield Q, since P & (P→Q) is just one value of 'P'.

So, to dismiss the suggestion, we need only be clear what it comes to, and we do not need to invoke a regress-argument. But it is not clear either that we are entitled to do so. The suggestion that we are depends upon thinking that if someone cavils at the argument 'A, B, ∴ Z' on the grounds that C is not one of its premises he is somehow committed to cavilling at 'A, B, C, ∴ Z' because C_2 is not one of *its* premises. But this is just wrong. If someone had a prejudice in favour of truth-functionally valid arguments he would be consistent in rejecting the first argument as invalid and then accepting the second. A critic who then asked to be satisfied that Z was legitimately drawn from A, B, and C would be shown a truth-table and that would be that. So there is no force in Ryle's suggestion that 'this new hypothetical (here, C_2) would have to be incorporated as a third component of a conjunctive premise'.

If all this is correct, then what is most usually taken to be established by the story, namely that we must not try to make the 'principle' of an inference one of its premises, on pain of running into an infinite regress, is wrong, and is not established by the story. What people who say this mean by taking the principle as one of the premises turns out to be what we called strengthening, and strengthening does not run us into a regress. The mistake of supposing that it does comes partly from failing to notice that the Tortoise changes his ground, shifts his difficulty, at the second stage. It is true that if someone thinks that every argument needs to be strengthened he will think or be committed to thinking that every argument is invalid, but to expose this we do not need to invoke a regress argument anyway. Neither does any such argument help us in seeing what needs to be seen, the way in which strengthening is either redundant or futile. The infinite regress is just an infinitely long red herring.

NOTES

1. *New Series*, vol. IV, pp. 278–80.

2. For example, an argument designed to show that such-and-such a book contains exactly one valid argument.

3. At least one writer on the story has been led to deny this. *See* D. G. Brown, '*What the Tortoise taught us*', *Mind*, vol. LXIII (1954), p. 179.

4. See the paper cited in the previous footnote.

5. In '*Philosophical Analysis*' edited by Max Black, New York, 1950.

QUESTIONS

I. LOGIC AND KNOWLEDGE

1. The tortoise asks Achilles to "force me, logically, to accept Z as true," but can anyone be logically forced to accept a proposition?

2. Does Rees's distinction between premises and meta-premises solve the problem of infinite regress?

3. Is Thompson correct that accepting a proposition is also agreeing to perform specific inferences from that proposition?

II

LOGIC AND
DEFINITION

The logical connectives—such as *and*, *or*, and *if/then*—can be defined *semantically* in terms of a truth table or *syntactically* by how they function within the rules of inference, such as *modus ponens* and *modus tollens*. The semantics and syntax for the connectives are supposed to complement each other.

But consider a new connective—*tonk*. We don't know the semantics for *tonk*, but it is governed by two familiar rules of inference: one analogous to the Addition rule (*p* entails *p or q*), the other analogous to the Simplification rule (*p and q* entails *q*). A. N. Prior explores the difficulties with any connective whose syntax is not constrained by semantics. J. I. Stevenson argues that any set of rules that define a connective must pass a semantic test of "complete justification." Nuel D. Belnap claims that the requirements provided by the semantic test can be captured by additional syntactic rules.

4

The Runabout Inference-Ticket

A. N. Prior

It is sometimes alleged that there are inferences whose validity arises solely from the meanings of certain expressions occurring in them. The precise technicalities employed are not important, but let us say that such inferences, if any such there be, are analytically valid.

One sort of inference which is sometimes said to be in this sense analytically valid is the passage from a conjunction to either of its conjuncts, e.g., the inference 'Grass is green and the sky is blue, therefore grass is green.' The validity of this inference is said to arise solely from the meaning of the word 'and.' For if we are asked what is the meaning of the word 'and,' at least in the purely conjunctive sense (as opposed to, e.g., its colloquial use to mean 'and then'), the answer is said to be *completely* given by saying that (i) from any pair of statements P and Q we can infer the statement formed by joining P to Q by 'and' (which statement we hereafter describe as 'the statement P-and-Q'), that (ii) from any conjunctive statement P-and-Q we can infer P, and (iii) from P-and-Q we can always infer Q. Anyone who has learnt to perform these inferences knows the meaning of 'and,' for there is simply nothing more *to* knowing the meaning of 'and' than being able to perform these inferences.

A doubt might be raised as to whether it is really the case that, for any pair of statements P and Q, there is always a statement R such that given P and given Q we can infer R, and given R we can infer P and can also infer Q. But on the view we are considering such a doubt is quite misplaced, once we have introduced a word, say the word 'and,' precisely in order to form a statement R with these properties from any pair of statements P and Q. The doubt reflects the old superstitious view that an expression must have some independently determined meaning before we can discover whether inferences involving it are valid or invalid. With analytically valid inferences this just isn't so.

I hope the conception of an analytically valid inference is now at least as clear to my readers as it is to myself. If not, further illumination is obtainable from Professor Popper's paper on 'Logic without Assumptions' in *Proceedings of the Aristotelian Society* for 1946–7, and from Professor Kneale's contribution to *Contemporary British Philosophy,* Volume III. I have also been much helped in my understanding of the notion by some lectures of Mr. Strawson's and some notes of Mr. Hare's.

I want now to draw attention to a point not generally noticed, namely that in this sense of 'analytically valid' any statement whatever may be inferred, in an analytically valid way, from any other. '2 and 2 are 5,' for instance, from '2 and 2 are 4.' It is done in two steps, thus:

- 2 and 2 are 4.
- Therefore, 2 and 2 are 4 tonk 2 and 2 are 5.
- Therefore, 2 and 2 are 5.

There may well be readers who have not previously encountered this conjunction 'tonk,' it being a comparatively recent addition to the language; but it is the simplest matter in the world to explain what it means. Its meaning is completely given by the rules that (i) from any statement P we can infer any statement formed by joining P to any statement Q by 'tonk' (which compound statement we hereafter describe as 'the statement P-tonk-Q'), and that (ii) from any 'contonktive' statement P-tonk-Q we can infer the contained statement Q.

A doubt might be raised as to whether it is really the case that, for any pair of statements P and Q, there is always a statement R such that given P we can infer R, and given R we can infer Q. But this doubt is of course quite misplaced, now that we have introduced the word 'tonk' precisely in order to form a statement R with these properties from any pair of statements P and Q.

As a matter of simple history, there have been logicians of some eminence who have seriously doubted whether sentences of the form 'P and Q' express single propositions (and so, e.g., have negations). Aristotle himself, in *De Soph. Elench.* 176 a 1 ff., denies that 'Are Callias and Themistocles musical?' is a single question; and J. S. Mill says of 'Caesar is dead and Brutus is alive' that 'we might as well call a street a complex house, as these two propositions a complex proposition' (*System of Logic* I, iv. 3). So it is not to be wondered at if the form 'P tonk Q' is greeted at first with similar scepticism. But more enlightened views will surely prevail at last, especially when men consider the extreme *convenience* of the new form, which promises to banish *falsche Spitfizndigkeit* from Logic for ever.

Roundabout the Runabout
Inference-Ticket

J. T. Stevenson

In his article "The Runabout Inference-Ticket" Professor A. N. Prior tries to show that there is an absurdity derivable from the theory ". . . that there are inferences whose validity arises solely from the meanings of certain expressions occurring in them."[1] For accounts of the theory other than his own Prior refers us to the writings of K. R. Popper, W. Kneale, P. F. Strawson, and R. M. Hare. I shall not be concerned to determine whether he has accurately represented their versions of the theory (although I think this doubtful for example in the case of Popper), because Prior's interpretation is itself intrinsically interesting. Prior's argument strongly suggests that there *is* something wrong with the theory, as he presents it, but, unfortunately, he does not show us *what* is wrong with it. I wish to show (1) exactly where the theory, *as stated by Prior,* goes wrong, and (2) that the theory can be stated in such a way as to be quite sound.

According to the theory in question, the inference 'Grass is green and the sky is blue, therefore grass is green' is an analytically valid inference solely in virtue of the meaning of the word 'and.' The presumed analyticity of the inference is exhibited by the following statement of the meaning of the word 'and': ". . . (i) from any pair of statements P

and Q we can infer the statement formed by joining P to Q by 'and' . . .
(ii) from any conjunctive statement P-and-Q we can infer P, and (iii)
from P-and-Q we can always infer Q."[2]

Prior attempts to reduce the foregoing theory to absurdity by introducing a new connective 'tonk' and giving it a meaning in the way suggested by the theory. The complete meaning of 'tonk' is: "(i) from any
statement P we can infer any statement formed by joining P to any statement Q by 'tonk' . . ., and . . . (ii) from any 'contonktive' statement P-
tonk-Q we can infer the contained statement statement Q."[3] He then
shows that the following inference is valid in virtue of the meaning of
'tonk':

> 2 and 2 are 4.
> Therefore, 2 and 2 are 4 tonk 2 and 2 are 5.
> Therefore, 2 and 2 are 5.[4]

Prior does not say, but seems to imply, this: Since the theory allows to
deduce, "in an analytically valid way", a patently false statement from
a patently true one, there must be something radically wrong with the
theory.

In order to understand what has happened here, it is essential to notice that the theory requires us to give the meaning of logical connectives in terms of *rules*. These rules are permissive: I take it that the
force of 'we can infer,' as it occurs in the foregoing definitions, is the
same as 'we *may* infer' or 'we are *allowed* or *permitted* to infer.' If 'we
can infer' were taken to mean the same as 'we may *validly* infer,' some
of the things I shall say would have to be modified. But, in this case, if
'valid' were used in its ordinary sense (namely, such as to lead from
truth only to truth and never to falsehood), Prior's definition of 'tonk'
would become radically incoherent, indeed self-contradictory, and his
argument trivially unsound and hence uninteresting. I shall take the

more interesting and more usual interpretation that rules of inference are simply permissive. Granted this, we can now consider two important insights and one serious error in the theory.

The first insight concerns the meaning of logical connectives: the way in which we can express the meaning of connectives must be different from the way in which we express the meanings of non-logical words. In the first place, leaving aside Platonism, connectives are not used to denote, and hence the sort of semantical properties they have will be different from those of non-logical words. Second, logical terms are syncategorematic or incomplete symbols; they have no meaning in isolation. Since the most distinctive feature of a logical term is its syntactical properties, we can explain its meaning to someone unfamiliar with it by exhibiting how these syntactical properties affect the contexts in which the connective in question occurs. And a very convenient way to do this is to give the permissive rules governing the inferences we can make using the connective.

The second insight is that we ordinarily justify (i.e., validate) inferences by appealing to a permissive rule. If you question my inference 'If I don't leave in five minutes, I shall be late, and I am not going to leave in five minutes; so I shall be late,' I justify it by appealing to the permissive rule *modus ponens.*

The serious error in the theory consists in combining these two insights in an unfortunate way. It is assumed that we can *completely* justify an inference by appealing to the meaning of a logical connective as stated in permissive rules. If this were so, we could, as Prior shows, justify any inference whatsoever by defining a logical connective in terms of permissive rules in such a way that we would be allowed to pass from true premises to a false conclusion.

The crucial point to be noted is this: in order to *completely* justify an inference we must appeal to a *sound* rule of inference. A complete justification of an inference has two parts: we must first *validate* the inference by subsuming it under a rule, and secondly we must *vindicate* the rule itself by showing that it is a sound rule.[5] A deductive rule is sound if and only if it permits only valid inferences, an inference being valid in this sense if and only if it is such that when the premises are true the conclusion must be true. The difficulty in our theory, then, is that it does not prevent us from defining connectives in terms of unsound permissive rules. Since no attempt is made to vindicate the rules used in the definitions, the definitions do not, by themselves, provide a complete justification of our inferences.

I now turn to the problem of stating the theory in such a way that it avoids the above difficulty. Basically, the theory states that certain inferences are completely justified solely in virtue of the meanings assigned to certain logical connectives. Since giving the meaning of a logical connective consists in giving its syntactical properties, we must show that, given a statement of the syntactical properties of a connective, the soundness of certain rules of inference can be demonstrated. There is no difficulty in doing this; it can be done, indeed, it has been done, for many different connectives, and there is no need to go into details here.[6]

To be more precise, two qualifications should be made. First: the syntactical properties of a connective include both its formation and transformation properties, although here only its transformation properties are considered. Second: we can exhibit the transformation properties of a sentence connective in a calculus by making a value-table for it either so that the calculus remains uninterpreted, or so that it becomes interpreted. In the former case, we might use some arbitrary symbols for the values (say 0 and 1), and deal with pure syntactical properties. In the latter case, we use truth and falsity as values; and, since truth is a semantical notion, the calculus becomes to some extent interpreted, and we are no longer dealing with pure syntactical proper-

ties. For answering questions of soundness the latter method is the one
which must be used; but for convenience I continue to speak simply of
syntactical properties.

In a formal calculus we can state the syntactical properties of, say, a
truth-functional binary sentence connective 'o,' by stating, in the meta-
language, the way in which the truth-value of the well-formed formula
'poq' is a function of (all possible combinations of) the truth-values of
the components 'p' and 'q.' We can then deduce from these statements,
in a very rigorous way, a meta-theorem of the calculus (again stated in
the meta-language) to the effect that such-and-such permissive rules
are sound, i.e., lead from truths only to truths and never to falsehoods.
Since from a statement of the meaning of a connective we can derive
demonstrably *sound* permissive rules of inference governing that connective, we may say that certain inferences are *completely* justified
solely in virtue of the meanings of certain expressions occurring in
them.

The important difference between the theory of analytic validity
as it should be stated and as Prior stated it lies in the fact that he gives
the meanings of connectives in terms of permissive rules, whereas
they should be stated in terms of truth-function statements in a meta-
language. The theory of analytic validity does *not* require that the
meanings of connectives be given in terms of rules; as we have seen,
to do so is to leave open the question of complete justification. What
the correct theory of analytic validity *does* require is that the meanings
of connectives be given in terms of statements of syntactical properties. When this is done the soundness of certain rules of inference is
demonstrable, and thus inferences can be completely justified by appealing to the meanings of connectives. Using the latter method we
block the introduction of a connective like Prior's 'tonk.' This can be
seen as follows.

Consider these two truth-tables which exhibit in a graphic way the syntactical properties of two binary sentence connectives 'o' and '§.'

A.	p	q	poq		B.	p	q	p§q
	T	T	T			T	T	T
	T	F	T			T	F	F
	F	T	F			F	T	T
	F	F	F			F	F	F

RA: p ∴ poq   RB: p§q ∴ q

From A it can be seen, intuitively, that the syntactical properties of 'o' permit us to demonstrate that the permissive rule RA, namely, from 'p' you may infer 'poq,' is sound; and with a properly formulated statement of these syntactical properties it can be rigorously demonstrated to be sound. Similarly, from B it can be seen that the rule RB, namely, from 'p§q' you may infer 'q,' is a sound rule. Prior's connective 'tonk' is governed by two rules like RA and RB. The syntactical properties of 'tonk,' then, must be a combination of the syntactical properties of 'o' and '§'; and in order to demonstrate the joint soundness of the rules for 'tonk,' we would have to construct a truth-table combining all the features of A and B. But it is obvious that this would involve ascribing contradictory syntactical properties to 'tonk.' This being so, it would be impossible to state consistently the meaning of 'tonk' in the manner I have suggested; and hence impossible to completely justify the inference from '2 and 2 are 4' to '2 and 2 are 5.' One could, of course, as Prior has done, state the meaning of 'tonk' in terms of rules and in this way justify (i.e., validate) '2 and 2 are 4, therefore, 2 and 2 are 5,' but this would not *completely* justify the inference, for it would leave open the question as to the *vindication* of the inference. And, of course, by definition it could never be vindicated, for it leads from an obvious truth to an obvious falsehood. I conclude, then, that there is nothing wrong with the theory of analytic validity when properly stated.[7]

NOTES

1. *Analysis* 21.2, December 1960.

2. *Ibid.*

3. *Ibid.*

4. *Ibid.*

5. The distinction between validation and vindication is due to H. Feigl. See "De Principiis non Disputandum . . . ?" in *Philosophical Analysis,* ed. Max Black (Cornell University Press, 1950).

6. See any standard text, e.g., Church's Introduction to Mathematical Logic.

7. I should like to acknowledge the benefit I have had of a number of stimulating discussions with Wesley C. Salmon on this topic. He is not, of course, responsible for any errors I may have made.

6

Tonk, Plonk and Plink[1]

Nuel D. Belnap

A. N. Prior has recently discussed[2] the connective *tonk,* where *tonk* is defined by specifying the role it plays in inference. Prior characterizes the role of *tonk* in inference by describing how it behaves as conclusion, and as premiss: (1) A $\vdash$ A-*tonk*-B, and (2) A-*tonk-B* $\vdash$ B (where we have used the sign ' $\vdash$ ' for deducibility). We are then led by the transitivity of deducibility to the validity of A $\vdash$ B, "which promises to banish *falsche Spitzfindigkeit* from Logic for ever."

A possible moral to be drawn is that connectives cannot be defined in terms of deducibility at all; that, for instance, it is illegitimate to define *and* as that connective such that (1) A-*and*-B $\vdash$ A, (2) A-*and*-B $\vdash$ B, and (3) A, B $\vdash$ A-*and*-B. We must first, so the moral goes, have a notion of what *and* means, independently of the role it plays as premiss and as conclusion. Truth-tables are one way of specifying this antecedent meaning; this seems to be the moral drawn by J. T. Stevenson.[3] There are good reasons, however, for defending the legitimacy of defining connections in terms of the roles they play in deductions.

It seems plain that throughout the whole texture of philosophy one can distinguish two modes of explanation: the analytic mode, which tends to explain wholes in terms of parts, and the synthetic mode, which explains parts in terms of the wholes or contexts in which they occur.[4] In logic, the analytic mode would be represented by Aristotle, who commences with terms as the ultimate atoms, explains propositions or judgments by means of these, syllogisms by means of the propositions which go to make them up, and finally ends with the notion of a science as a tissue of syllogisms. The analytic mode is also represented by the contemporary logician who first explains the meaning of complex sentences, by means of truth-tables, as a function of their parts, and then proceeds to give an account of correct inference in terms of the sentences occurring therein. The *locus classicus* of the application of the synthetic mode is, I suppose, Plato's treatment of justice in the *Republic,* where he defines the just man by reference to the larger context of the community. Among formal logicians, use of the synthetic mode in logic is illustrated by Kneale and Popper (cited by Prior), as well as by Jaskowski, Gentzen, Fitch, and Curry, all of these treating the meaning of connectives as arising from the role they play in the context of formal inference. It is equally well illustrated, I think, by aspects of Wittgenstein and those who learned from him to treat the meanings of words as arising from the role they play in the context of discourse. It seems to me nearly self-evident that employment of both modes of explanation is important and useful. It would therefore be truly a shame to see the synthetic mode in logic pass away as a result of a severe attack of tonktitis.

Suppose, then, that we wish to hold that it is after all possible to define connectives contextually, in terms of deducibility. How are we to prevent tonktitis? How are we to make good the claim that there is no connective such as *tonk*[5] though there is a connective such as *and* (where *tonk* and *and* are defined as above)?

It seems to me that the key to a solution[6] lies in observing that even on the synthetic view, we are not defining our connectives *ab initio*, but rather in terms of an *antecedently given context of deducibility*, concerning which we have some definite notions. By that I mean that before arriving at the problem of characterizing connectives, we have already made some assumptions about the nature of deducibility. That this is so can be seen immediately by observing Prior's use of the transitivity of deducibility in order to secure his ingenious result. But if we note that we already *have* some assumptions about the context of deducibility within which we are operating, it becomes apparent that by a too careless use of definitions, it is possible to create a situation in which we are forced to say things inconsistent with those assumptions.

The situation is thus exactly analogous to that, pointed out by Peano, which occurs when one attempts to define an operation, '?', on rational numbers as follows:

$$\left(\frac{a}{b} \; ? \; \frac{c}{d} \right) =_{df} \frac{a + c}{b + d}.$$

This definition is inadmissible precisely because it has consequences which contradict prior assumptions; for, as can easily be shown, admitting this definition would lead to (say) $\frac{2}{3} = \frac{3}{5}$.

In short, we can distinguish between the admissibility of the definition of *and* and the inadmissibility of *tonk* on the grounds of consistency—*i.e.,* consistency with antecedent assumptions. We can give a precise account of the requirement of consistency from the synthetic point of view as follows.

(1) We consider some characterization of deducibility, which may be treated as a formal system, *i.e.,* as a set of axioms and rules involving the sign of deducibility, ' $\vdash$ ', where '$A_1, \ldots, A_n \vdash B$' is read 'B is deducible

from $A_1, \ldots, A_n$' For definiteness, we shall choose as our characterization the structural rules of Gentzen:

Axiom. $A \vdash A$

Rules.   *Weakening*:   from $A_1, \ldots, A_n \vdash C$
                          to infer $A_1, \ldots, A_n B \vdash C$

          Permutation: from $A_1, \ldots, A_i, A_{i+1}, \ldots, A_n \vdash B$
                          to infer $A_1, \ldots, A_{i+1}, A_i, \ldots, A_n \vdash B$.

          Contraction: from $A_1, \ldots, A_n, A_n \vdash B$
                          to infer $A_1, \ldots, A_n \vdash B$

          Transitivity: from $A_1, \ldots, A_m \vdash B$
                          and $C_1, \ldots, C_n, B \vdash D$
                          to infer $A_1, \ldots, A_m, C_1, \ldots, C_n \vdash D$.

In accordance with the opinions of experts (or even perhaps on more substantial grounds) we may take this little system as expressing all and only the universally valid statements and rules expressible in the given notation: it completely determines the context.

(2) We may consider the proposed definition of some connective, say *plonk*, as an *extension* of the formal system characterizing deducibility, and an extension in two senses, (a) The notion of sentence is extended by introducing A-*plonk*-B as a sentence, whenever A and B are sentences. (b) We add some axioms or rules governing A-*plonk*-B as occurring as one of the premises or as conclusion of a deducibility-statement. These axioms or rules constitute our definition of *plonk* in terms of the role it plays in inference.

(3) We may now state the demand for the consistency of the definition of the new connective, *plonk*, as follows: the extension must be *conservative*[7]; *i.e.,* although the extension may well have new deducibility-statements, these new statements will all involve *plonk*. The extension

will not have any new deducibility-statements which do not involve *plonk* itself. It will not lead to any deducibility-statement $A_1, \ldots, A_n \vdash$ B not containing *plonk*, unless that statement is already provable in the absence of *plonk*-axioms *plonk*-rules. The justification for unpacking the demand for consistency in terms of conservativeness is precisely our antecedent assumption that we already had *all* the universally valid deducibility-statements not involving any special connectives.

So the trouble with the definition of *tonk* given by Prior is that it is inconsistent. It gives us an extension of our original characterization of deducibility which is not conservative, since in the extension (but not in the original) we have, for arbitrary A and B, $A \vdash B$. Adding a tonkish role to the deducibility-context would be like adding to cricket a player whose role was so specified as to make it impossible to distinguish winning from losing.

Hence, given that our characterization of deducibility is taken as complete, we may with propriety say 'There is no such connective as *tonk*'; just as we say that there is no operation, '?', on rational numbers such that $\left(\frac{a}{b} \; ? \; \frac{c}{d} \right) \; = \; \frac{a + c}{b + d}$. On the other hand, it is easily shown that the extension got by adding *and* is conservative, and we may hence say 'There *is* a connective having these properties.'

It is good to keep in mind that the question of the existence of a connective having such and such properties is relative to our characterization of deducibility. If we had initially allowed $A \vdash B$ (!), there would have been no objection to *tonk*, since the extension would then have been conservative. Also, there would have been no inconsistency had we omitted from our characterization of deducibility the rule of transitivity.

The mathematical analogy leads us to ask if we ought not also to add *uniqueness*[8] as a requirement for connectives introduced by definitions in terms of deducibility (although clearly this requirement is not as essential as the first, or at least not in the same way). Suppose, for example, that I propose to define a connective *plonk* by specifying that B $\vdash$ A-*plonk*-B. The extension is easily shown to be conservative, and we may, therefore, say 'There is a connective having these properties.' But is there only one? It seems rather odd to say we have defined *plonk* unless we can show that A-*plonk*-B is a function of A and B, *i.e.,* given A and B, there is only one proposition A-*plonk*-B. But what do we mean by uniqueness when operating from a synthetic, contextualist point of view? Clearly that at most *one* inferential role is permitted by the characterization of *plonk*; *i.e.,* that there cannot be two connectives which share the characterization given to *plonk* but which otherwise sometimes play different roles. Formally put, uniqueness means that if exactly the same properties are ascribed to some other connective, say *plink*, then A-*plink*-B will play exactly the same role in inference as A-*plonk*-B, both as premiss and as conclusion. To say that *plonk* (characterized thus and so) describes a unique way of combining A and B is to say that if *plink* is given a characterization formally identical to that of *plonk*, then

(1) $A_1, \ldots, B\text{-}plonk\text{-}C, \ldots, A_n \vdash D$ if and only if
        $A_1, \ldots, B\text{-}plink\text{-}C, \ldots, A_n \vdash D$

and

(2) $A_1, \ldots, A_n \vdash B\text{-}plonk\text{-}C$ if and only if $A_1, \ldots, A_n \vdash B\text{-}plink\text{-}C.$

Whether or not we can show this will depend, of course, not only on the properties ascribed to the connectives, but also on the properties ascribed to deducibility. Given the characterization of deducibility above, it is sufficient and necessary that B-*plonk*-C $\vdash$ B-*plink*-C, and conversely.

Harking back now to the definition of *plonk* by: B $\vdash$ A-*plonk*-B, it is easy to show that *plonk* is *not* unique; that given only: B $\vdash$ A-*plonk*-B, and B $\vdash$ A-*plink*-B, we cannot show that *plonk* and *plink* invariably play the same role in inference. Hence, the possibility arises that *plonk* and *plink* stand for different connectives: the conditions *on plonk* do not determine a unique connective. On the other hand, if we introduce a connective, *et*, with the same characterization as *and*, it will turn out that A-*and*-B and A-*et*-B play exactly the same role in inference. The conditions on *and* therefore do determine a unique connective.

Though it is difficult to draw a moral from Prior's delightful note without being plonking, I suppose we might put it like this: one *can* define connectives in terms of deducibility, but one bears the onus of proving at least consistency (existence); and if one wishes further to talk about *the* connective (instead of *a* connective) satisfying certain conditions, it is necessary to prove uniqueness as well. But it is not necessary to have an antecedent idea of the independent meaning of the connective.

NOTES

1. This research was supported in part by the Office of Naval Research, Group Psychology Branch, Contract No. SAR/Nonr-609(16).

2. 'The Runabout Inference-ticket,' *Analysis* 21.2, December 1960.

3. 'Roundabout the Runabout Inference-ticket,' *Analysis* 21.6, June 1961. Cf. p. 127: "The important difference between the theory of analytic validity [Prior's phrase for what is here called the synthetic view] as it should be stated and as Prior stated it lies in the fact that he gives the meaning of connectives in terms of permissive rules, whereas they should be stated in terms of truth-function statements in a meta-language."

4. I learned this way of looking at the matter from R. S. Brumbaugh.

5. That there is no meaningful proposition expressed by A-*tonk*-B; that there is no meaningful sentence A-*tonk*-B—distinctions suggested by these alternative modes of expression are irrelevant. Not myself being a victim of eidophobia, I will continue to use language which treats the connective-word '*tonk*' as standing for the putative propositional connective, *tonk*. It is equally irrelevant whether we take the sign $\vdash$ as representing a syntactic concept of deducibility or a semantic concept of logical consequence.

6. Prior's note is a gem, reminding one of Lewis Carroll's 'What the Tortoise said to Achilles.' And as for the latter, so for the former, I suspect that no solution will ever be universally accepted as *the* solution.

7. The notion of conservative extensions is due to Emil Post.

8. Application to connectives of the notions of existence and uniqueness was suggested to me by a lecture of H. Hiż.

QUESTIONS

II. LOGIC AND DEFINITION

1. According to Prior, what is a runabout inference-ticket?

2. According to Belnap what is tonkitis?

3. Are the laws of logic merely conventional?

III

LOGIC AND INFERENCE

Vann McGee presents what he takes to be a counterexample to *modus ponens*. Suppose you are reading *The Odyssey*. Suppose further that if you are reading *The Odyssey*, then if you are reading the first book, you are reading about Telemachus and Penelope. These premises seem to entail that *if you are reading the first book, then you are reading about Telemachus.* Yet this conclusion may not be true. You could be reading the first book of the *Iliad,* and so you are reading about Achilles and Brisias; or you might be reading the first book of the Bible, and so you would be reading about Adam and Eve.

E. J. Lowe suggests that "if" clauses are intrinsically ambiguous in the English language and that McGee's proposed counterexample can be defused with a more careful translation from the English sentences into logical notation. D. E. Over contends that the context of statement, *if you are reading the first book, then you are reading about Telemachus,* makes clear that the statement is true of the specific book you are reading and not just any book.

A Counterexample to Modus Ponens[1]

Vann McGee

The rule of *modus ponens*, which tells us that from an indicative conditional ⌜If ϕ then ψ⌝,[2] together with its antecedent ϕ, one can infer ψ, is one of the fundamental principles of logic.[3] Yet, as the following examples show, it is not strictly valid; there are occasions on which one has good grounds for believing the premises of an application of modus ponens but yet one is not justified in accepting the conclusion. Later on, we shall see how these examples can be modified to give counterexamples to Stalnaker's semantics for the conditional:

Opinion polls taken just before the 1980 election showed the Republican Ronald Reagan decisively ahead of the Democrat Jimmy Carter, with the other Republican in the race, John Anderson, a distant third. Those apprised of the poll results believed, with good reason:

If a Republican wins the election, then if it's not Reagan who wins it will be Anderson.
A Republican will win the election.

Yet they did not have reason to believe

If it's not Reagan who wins, it will be Anderson.

I see what looks like a large fish writhing in a fisherman's net a
ways off. I believe

If that creature is a fish, then if it has lungs, it's a lungfish.

That, after all, is what one means by "lungfish." Yet, even though I
believe the antecedent of this conditional, I do not conclude

If that creature has lungs, it's a lungfish.

Lungfishes are rare, oddly shaped, and, to my knowledge, appear
only in fresh water. It is more likely that, even though it does not
look like one, the animal in the net is a porpoise.

Having learned that gold and silver were both once mined in his
region, Uncle Otto has dug a mine in his backyard. Unfortunately,
it is virtually certain that he will find neither gold nor silver, and it
is entirely certain that he will find nothing else of value. There is
ample reason to believe

If Uncle Otto doesn't find gold, then if he strikes it rich, it
will be by finding silver.
Uncle Otto won't find gold.

Since, however, his chances of finding gold, though slim, are no
slimmer than his chances of finding silver, there is no reason to suppose that

If Uncle Otto strikes it rich, it will be by finding silver.

These examples show that modus ponens is not an entirely reliable rule of inference. Sometimes the conclusion of an application of modus ponens is something we do not believe and should not believe, even though the premises are propositions we believe very properly.[4]

Modus ponens is sometimes thought of not as a rule of inference but as a law of semantics, to wit, whenever ⌜If ϕ then ψ⌝ and ϕ are both true, ψ is true as well. It is not at all obvious what we are to make of this law, since it is not evident what the truth conditions for the English conditional are or even whether it has truth conditions. Still it seems unlikely that, even if we learned the truth conditions for the English conditional, the semantic version of modus ponens would be vindicated. Let us imagine, on the contrary, that some time in the future linguists will determine the truth conditions for the English conditional and prove that modus ponens is truth-preserving. Assuming that basic zoology will not have changed, a future linguist who sees what looks like a large fish writhing in a fisherman's net a ways off will believe, as I believed,

> If that animal is a fish, then if it has lungs it's a lungfish.
> That animal is a fish.

Suppose he also believes this:

> It is true that, if that animal is a fish, then if it has lungs it's a lungfish.
> It is true that that animal is a fish.

Then he will be able to prove, using the well-established principle of future semantics that modus ponens is truth-preserving:

> It is true that, if that animal has lungs, it is a lungfish.

He will not, however, believe

> If that animal has lungs, it is a lungfish.

any more than I did. Thus our future linguist will be either in the awkward position of believing the premises of the argument without believing that those premises are true, or else in the equally awkward
position of not believing the conclusion of the argument even though
he does believe that that conclusion is true.[5] Thus the only way that we
can hold on to the doctrine that modus ponens is truth-preserving will
be to accept an unexpected disparity between believing a proposition
and believing that that proposition is true.

In an attempt to supply truth conditions where nature provides none,
philosophers have settled upon material implication: Count $\ulcorner$If ϕ then
$\psi\urcorner$ as true if either ϕ is false or ψ is true. Sometimes this is intended as
a proposal for linguistic reform, a suggestion that, at least in our scientific discourse, we ought to use the "If-then" construction in a new way,
treating it as the material conditional rather than the ordinary conditional. Our examples do not raise any difficulties for this proposal, since
if we reinterpret them this way, our examples become arguments with
true premises and true conclusions. Sometimes, however, material implication is proposed as an account of how we presently use the "If-
then" construction. This is surely wrong. If we have seen the polls
showing Reagan far ahead of Carter, who is far ahead of Anderson, we
will not for a moment suppose that

> If Reagan doesn't win, Anderson will.

is true, even though we will resign ourselves to the truth of

> Reagan will win.

Our counterexamples to modus ponens have a characteristic logical form. Each has as a premise a conditional whose consequent is itself a conditional. In general, we assert, accept, or believe a conditional of the form ⌜If ϕ, then if ψ then ϕ⌝ whenever we are willing to assert, accept, or believe the conditional ⌜If ϕ and ψ, then θ⌝ . It appears, from looking at examples, that the law of exportation.

⌜If ϕ and ψ, then θ ⌝ entails ⌜If ϕ, then if ψ then θ ⌝.

is a feature of English usage.[6] If so, then our counterexamples to modus ponens are not isolated curiosities but rather symptoms of a basic difficulty. It is natural to suppose that the English indicative conditional is intermediate in strength between strict implication and material implication. That is to say, whenever ψ is a logical consequence of ϕ, ⌜If ϕ then ψ⌝ will be true, and whenever ⌜If ϕ then ψ⌝ is true, either ϕ will be false or ψ true (and so modus ponens is truth-preserving). It now appears that we also want to require that the law of exportation be valid. But there is no connective other than the material conditional that meets all these requirements.

Theorem. Suppose that we have a logical consequence relation $\vdash$ on a language whose connectives comprise the ordinary Boolean connectives '$\vee$', '$\&$', '$\sim$', '$\supset$', and '$\equiv$', as well as an additional conditional '$\Rightarrow$', satisfying the following conditions:

(Cons) $\vdash$, a relation between sets of sentences and sentences, is a consequence relation:

If $\phi \in \Gamma$, then $\Gamma \vdash \phi$

If $\Gamma \vdash \phi$ and $\Gamma \subseteq \Delta$, then $\Delta \vdash \phi$.

If $\Delta \vdash \psi$ for each $\psi \in \Gamma$ and $\Gamma \vdash \phi$, then $\Delta \vdash \phi$.

(Exp)   The law of exportation for "$\Rightarrow$":

$\{ ⌜\phi \& \psi \Rightarrow \theta ⌝ \} \vdash ⌜\phi \Rightarrow (\psi \Rightarrow \theta)⌝$.

(MP)   Modus ponens for both conditionals "$\Rightarrow$" and "$\supset$":

$$\{\ulcorner \phi \Rightarrow \psi \urcorner , \phi\} \vdash \psi$$

$$\{\ulcorner \phi \supset \psi \urcorner , \phi\} \vdash \psi$$

(StrImp)   Strict implication is as strong or stronger than either
conditional: If $\{\phi\} \vdash \psi$, then $\Phi \vdash \ulcorner \phi \Rightarrow \psi \urcorner$ and
$\Phi \vdash \ulcorner \phi \supset \psi \urcorner$ (where Φ is the empty set).

(Taut)   Ordinary Boolean connectives behave normally:
If ϕ is a tautology,[7] then $\Phi \vdash \phi$.[8]

Then the two conditionals "$\Rightarrow$" and "$\supset$" are logically indistinguishable. More precisely, if ϕ and ϕ' are alike except that '$\Rightarrow$' and '$\supset$' have
been exchanged at some places, then $\{\phi\} \vdash \phi'$ and $\{\phi'\} \vdash \phi$.

The idea of the proof, which proceeds by induction on the complexity
of ϕ, is contained in the proof that $\{\ulcorner \psi \supset \theta \urcorner\} \vdash \ulcorner \psi \Rightarrow \theta \urcorner$:[9]

(i) $\Phi \vdash \ulcorner ((\psi \supset \theta) \,\&\, \psi) \supset \theta \urcorner$ by (Taut).

(ii) $\{\ulcorner ((\psi \supset \theta) \,\&\, \psi) \supset \theta \urcorner ; \ulcorner (\psi \supset \theta) \,\&\, \psi \urcorner\} \vdash \theta$ by (MP) for '$\supset$'

(iii) $\{\ulcorner (\psi \supset \theta) \,\&\, \psi \urcorner\} \vdash \theta$ from (i) and (ii) by (Cons)

(iv) $\Phi \vdash \ulcorner ((\psi \supset \theta) \,\&\, \psi \Rightarrow \theta \urcorner$ from (iii) by (StrImp) for '$\Rightarrow$'

(v) $\{\ulcorner ((\psi \supset \theta) \,\&\, \psi) \Rightarrow \theta \urcorner\} \vdash \ulcorner (\psi \supset \theta) \Rightarrow (\psi \Rightarrow \theta) \urcorner$ by (Exp)

(vi) $\{\ulcorner (\psi \supset \theta) \Rightarrow (\psi \Rightarrow \theta) \urcorner ; \ulcorner \psi \supset \theta \urcorner\} \vdash \ulcorner \psi \Rightarrow \theta \urcorner$
by (MP) for '$\Rightarrow$'

(vii) $\{\ulcorner \psi \supset \theta \urcorner\} \vdash \ulcorner \psi \Rightarrow \theta \urcorner$ from (iv), (v), and (vi) by (Cons)

The theorem points to a tension between modus ponens and the law
of exportation. According to the classical account, which does not recognize any conditional other than the material, both are valid; but we
will not expect them both to come out valid on any nonclassical account.

We have explicit examples to show that the indicative conditional
does not satisfy modus ponens. It is not so easy to test whether the rule

is valid for the subjunctive conditional, since we seldom use the subjunctive conditional in situations in which we are confident that the antecedent is true. On the other hand, it is easy to find natural instances of the law of exportation that employ the subjunctive mood; for example,

> If Juan hadn't married Xochitl and Sylvia hadn't run off to India, Juan and Sylvia would have become lovers.

entails

> If Juan hadn't married Xochitl, then if Sylvia hadn't run off to India, Juan and Sylvia would have become lovers.

Multiplying such examples, we get good inductive evidence that the subjunctive conditional satisfies the law of exportation. If this evidence is correct, then no theory of the subjunctive conditional which denies the law of exportation will be entirely accurate. The most prominent logical theory of the subjunctive conditional is Robert Stalnaker's account,[10] according to which we test whether $\ulcorner \phi \Rightarrow \psi \urcorner$ is true in a possible world ω by seeing whether ψ is true in the possible world most similar to ω in which ϕ is true. Stalnaker's system satisfies conditions (Cons), (MP), (StrImp), and (Taut), but it does not satisfy the law of exportation. Thus we are led to suspect that Stalnaker's analysis of the subjunctive conditional is inaccurate.

Concrete examples confirm our suspicions. We would ordinarily say (at least in contexts in which we are interested in the election results rather than, say, how else the primaries might have turned out),

> If Reagan hadn't won the election and a Republican had won, it would have been Anderson.

Appropriately, the Stalnaker semantics, under the natural comparitive similarity ordering among worlds, has this sentence come out true. As the law of exportation predicts, we also want to say,

> If Reagan hadn't won the election, then if a Republican had won, it would have been Anderson.

However, the possible world most similar to the actual world in which Reagan did not win the election will be a world in which Carter finished first and Reagan second, with Anderson again a distant third, and so a world in which "If a Republican had won it would have been Reagan" is true. Thus Stalnaker's theory wrongly predicts that, in the actual world,

> If Reagan hadn't won the election, then if a Republican had won, it would have been Reagan.

will be true. Thus, in this instance, the law of exportation is right and the Stalnaker semantics is wrong.

Another example: Let us imagine that, contrary to all our expectations, Uncle Otto finds a rich vein of gold, deeply buried in a distant corner of his property. We still believe this:

> If Uncle Otto hadn't found gold but he had struck it rich, it would have been by finding silver.

We also believe, as the law of exportation predicts,

> If Uncle Otto hadn't found gold, then if he had struck it rich, it would have been by finding silver.

What does the Stalnaker semantics say? The closest world to the actual world in which Uncle Otto does not find gold—call it ω—will be a world in which the deposit of gold is located just on the other side of Otto's property line, or perhaps a world in which Otto does not dig quite deeply enough to reach the vein. The world closest to ω in which Otto strikes it rich will be a world in which the gold is relocated back onto Otto's property and Otto digs deeply enough to find the gold. Thus the closest world to ω in which Uncle Otto strikes it rich will be a world in which

> Uncle Otto finds gold.

is true. Therefore, in ω,

> If Uncle Otto had struck it rich, it would have been by finding gold

is true, and so, according to Stalnaker's semantics,

> If Uncle Otto hadn't found gold, then if he had struck it rich, it would have been by finding gold.

is true in the actual world. Once again, the law of exportation scores a point against the Stalnaker semantics.

Our examples show us that an accurate logic for the English indicative conditional would have to restrict the rule of modus ponens somehow, and they suggest that the same would be true of an accurate logic of the subjunctive conditional. Nevertheless, all the familiar logics of the conditional countenance modus ponens without reservations. How do we account for this discrepancy? The simplest diagnosis is that we have committed an error of overly hasty generalization. We encounter a great many conditionals in daily life, and we have noticed that, when we accept a conditional and we accept its antecedent, we are prone to accept the consequent as well. We have supposed that this pattern held universally, with no exceptions. However, the examples we looked at were nearly always examples of simple conditionals, conditionals that did not themselves contain conditionals. Indeed there is every reason to suppose that, restricted to such conditionals, modus ponens is unexceptionable. But when we turn our attention to compound conditionals, new phenomena appear, and patterns that established themselves in the simple cases are disrupted.

The methodological moral to be drawn from this is that, when we formulate general laws of logic, we ought to exercise the same sort of caution we exercise when we make inductive generalizations in the empirical sciences. We must take care that the instances we look at in evaluating a proposed generalization are diverse as well as numerous.

It is perhaps surprising that, in constructing a logical theory, one comes upon the same pitfalls one encounters in the empirical sciences, since it is widely believed that logic is an a priori science. Upon reflection, however, we see that there is no cause for perplexity. If one believes that the correctness of a logically valid inference is recognized by an a priori intuition, what one believes is this:

> If $\Re$ is a valid rule of inference, then whenever R is an instance of $\Re$, one can see by an a priori intuition that R is a correct inference.

In order to conclude that the general laws of logic can be established purely by a priori reasoning, we would have to know something stronger, namely,

> If $\Re$ is a valid rule of inference, then one can see by an a priori
> intuition that, whenever R is an instance of $\Re$, R is a correct
> inference.

Our examples show that modus ponens is not strictly valid. They do nothing to dissuade us from our entrenched belief that modus ponens is valid for simple conditionals. They suggest that the law of exportation is valid for a wide range of cases, perhaps even valid universally. Beyond this, the examples give us no positive guidance toward constructing a correct logic of conditionals. It may be that some entirely new approach is needed, but it may also be that we can modify some existing theory to take the examples into account.

It is not hard to modify the Stalnaker semantics so that it has the right logical features. Instead of the simple notion of truth in a world, we develop a notion of truth in a world under a set of hypotheses. To be simply true in a world is to be true in that world under the empty set of hypotheses. If there is no world accessible from ω in which all the members of Γ are true, then every sentence is true in ω under the set of hypotheses Γ. Otherwise we have the following: An atomic sentence is true in ω under the set of hypotheses Γ iff it is true in the possible world most similar to ω in which all the members of Γ are true. A conjunction is true in a world under a given set of hypotheses if each of its conjuncts is. A disjunction is true in a world under a set of hypotheses iff one or both disjuncts are. $\ulcorner \sim \phi \urcorner$ is true in ω under the set of hypotheses Γ iff ϕ is not true in ω under that set of hypotheses. Finally, $\ulcorner \phi \Rightarrow \psi \urcorner$ is true in ω under the set of hypotheses Γ iff ψ is true in ω under the set of hypotheses $\Gamma \cup \{\phi\}$. Thus to evaluate whether $\ulcorner \phi \Rightarrow (\psi \Rightarrow \theta) \urcorner$ is true under the set of hypotheses Γ, we add first ϕ and then ψ to our set of hypotheses, and we see whether θ is true under the augmented set of hypotheses $\Gamma \cup \{\phi, \psi\}$. This semantics gives a logic that is compact and decidable.

For each sentence constructed using this modified Stalnaker conditional, we can find a logically equivalent sentence that uses the original Stalnaker conditional. We use '$\Rightarrow$' to stand for the modified Stalnaker conditional and '$>$' to denote the connective Stalnaker originally described. We take the Boolean connectives to be '$\vee$', '$\&$', '$\sim$', and a logically constant false sentence '$\perp$'. Define the operation * by:

$\phi^* = \phi$ if ϕ is an atomic sentence.

'$\perp$'$^* =$ '$\perp$'

$\ulcorner (\phi \vee \psi) \urcorner^* = \ulcorner (\phi^* \vee \psi^*) \urcorner$

$\ulcorner (\phi \,\&\, \psi) \urcorner^* = \ulcorner (\phi^* \,\&\, \psi^*) \urcorner$

$\ulcorner \sim \phi \urcorner = \ulcorner \sim (\phi^*) \urcorner$

$\ulcorner (\phi \Rightarrow \psi) \urcorner^* = \ulcorner (\phi^* > \psi^*) \urcorner$ if ψ is an atomic sentence or '$\perp$'

$\ulcorner (\phi \Rightarrow (\psi \vee \theta)) \urcorner^* = \ulcorner ((\phi \Rightarrow \psi)^* \vee (\phi \Rightarrow \theta)^*) \urcorner$

$\ulcorner (\phi \Rightarrow (\psi \,\&\, \theta)) \urcorner^* = \ulcorner ((\phi \Rightarrow \psi)^* \,\&\, (\phi \Rightarrow \theta)^*) \urcorner$

$\ulcorner (\phi \Rightarrow \sim \psi) \urcorner^* = \ulcorner ((\phi \Rightarrow \perp)^* \vee \sim ((\phi \Rightarrow \psi)^*)) \urcorner$

$\ulcorner (\phi \Rightarrow (\psi \Rightarrow \theta)) \urcorner^* = \ulcorner ((\phi \,\&\, \psi) \Rightarrow \theta) \urcorner^*$

ϕ and ϕ^* are logically equivalent.

Another approach we might use would be to continue to use a formal system in which modus ponens has unrestricted validity, and to take account of the invalidity of modus ponens in English by modifying our informal rules for translating English sentences into the formal language.[11] Thus we do not translate an English sentence of the form $\ulcorner$If ϕ, then if ψ then $\theta \urcorner$; in the natural way, as a formula of the form $\ulcorner (\phi \Rightarrow (\psi \Rightarrow \theta)) \urcorner$; instead we translate it as $\ulcorner ((\phi \,\&\, \psi) \Rightarrow \theta) \urcorner$. Thus the invalid English inference:

If ϕ, then if ψ then θ.

ϕ.

Therefore if ψ then θ.

is translated as the invalid formal inference:

$(\phi \,\&\, \psi) \Rightarrow \theta$.

ϕ.

Therefore $\psi \Rightarrow \theta$.

It is sometimes a bit arbitrary whether to account for a feature of English usage within our formal system or to account for it at the informal level of translation lore. For example, we just discussed a way of modifying the Stalnaker conditional so as to make the law of exportation generally valid. If we let $\mathrm{Tr}(\phi)$ be the "natural" translation of an English sentence ϕ into a formal language whose connectives are the Boolean connectives and '$\Rightarrow$', we can equally well take the translation of ϕ to be $\mathrm{Tr}(\phi)$ and use the modified Stalnaker semantics or take the translation of ϕ to be $(\mathrm{Tr}(\phi))^*$ and use the original Stalnaker semantics.

The selective use of unnatural translations is a powerful technique for improving the fit between the logic of the natural language and the logic of a formal language. In fact, it is a little too powerful. One suspects that, if one is sly enough in giving translations, one can enable almost any logic to survive almost any counterexample. What is needed is a systematic account of how to give the translations. In the absence of such an account, the unnatural translations will seem like merely an ad hoc device for evading counterexamples.

There is no guarantee that any approach will work. It may be that it is not possible to give a satisfactory logic of conditionals. This is not to say that it is not possible to give a linguistic account of how we use conditionals, but only to say that such an account would not give rise to a tractable theory of logical consequence.

NOTES

1. I would like to thank Ernest Adams for his great help in preparing this paper. He read the paper carefully and made a number of thoughtful and valuable suggestions.

2. The corners, ' $\ulcorner$ ' and ' $\urcorner$ ', are quasi-quotation marks. See Willard Van Orman Quine, *Mathematical Logic* (New York: Norton, 1940; Harper & Row, 1951), pp. 33–37.

3. Here I speak of inferring the sentence ψ from the sentences $\ulcorner$If ϕ then $\psi\urcorner$ and ϕ, and at other places I shall speak of inferring the proposition ψ from the propositions $\ulcorner$If ϕ then $\psi\urcorner$ and ϕ. It would be more precise, but also more tedious, to say that we infer the proposition expressed by the sentence ψ from the propositions expressed by the sentences $\ulcorner$If ϕ then $\psi\urcorner$ and ϕ.

4. There are, of course, familiar cases in which we see that an application of modus ponens leads us from premises we reasonably believe to a conclusion we find utterly incredible, and we respond by repudiating the premises rather than accepting the conclusion. The present examples are not like this, since we do not renounce the premises.

5. The first horn of this dilemma would not be uncomfortable to someone like Adams [*The Logic of Conditionals* (Boston: Reidel, 1975)] who doubts that conditionals are either true or false. By hypothesis, this is not the situation of our future linguist.

6. It would appear that the law of importation, the converse of the law of exportation, is also valid.

7. To see whether ϕ is a tautology, apply the following test: First replace every sub-formula of ϕ of the form $\ulcorner\psi \Rightarrow \theta\urcorner$ that is not itself contained in such a subformula by a new sentential letter. Then apply the usual truth-table test.

8. We get an equivalent set of conditions by replacing (Exp) and (StrImp) for '$\Rightarrow$' by the principle

(Cond) If $[\Gamma] \cup \{\phi\} \vdash \psi$, then $\Gamma \vdash \ulcorner \phi \Rightarrow \psi \urcorner$.

This rule reflects the way we customarily prove conditionals: Add ϕ hypothetically to our body of theory. If we can prove ψ in the augmented theory, count $\ulcorner$ If ϕ then $\psi \urcorner$ as proved.

9. This conclusion already shows us that '$\Rightarrow$' is not genuinely stronger than the material conditional, as we would have hoped. Notice that to get it we need only this very weak form of (StrImp):

If ψ is a tautological consequence of ϕ, then $\Phi \vdash \ulcorner \phi \Rightarrow \psi \urcorner$.

10. "A Theory of Conditionals," in Nicholas Rescher, ed., *Studies in Logical Theory. American Philosophical Quarterly* supplementary monograph series (Oxford: Blackwell, 1968), pp. 98–112.

11. Barry Loewer, "Counterfactuals with Disjunctive Antecedents," this *Journal*, LXXIII, 16 (Sept. 16, 1976): 531–537, has proposed using this strategy for coping with a different difficulty with Stalnaker's analysis.

Not a Counterexample to Modus Ponens

E. J. Lowe

In 'A Counterexample to Modus Ponens' (*The Journal of Philosophy* LXXXII, 9, September 1985, pp. 462–71), Vann McGee presents the following alleged counterexample to *modus ponens* (he also presents two others which, however, are constructed in essentially the same way):

> Opinion polls taken just before the 1980 election showed the Republican Ronald Reagan decisively ahead of the Democrat Jimmy Carter, with the other Republican in the race, John Anderson, a distant third. Those apprised of the polls results believed, with good reason:
>
>> If a Republican wins the election, then if it's not Reagan who wins it will be Anderson.
>> A Republican will win the election.
>
> Yet they did not have reason to believe
>
>> If it's not Reagan who wins, it will be Anderson. (p. 462)

The example fails to serve McGee's purpose because, I believe, it does not exhibit a genuine application of *modus ponens*—a rule which, in McGee's own words, 'tells us that from an indicative conditional $\ulcorner$If ϕ then $\psi\urcorner$, together with its antecedent ϕ, one can infer ψ' (ibid.). McGee clearly supposes that his example supplies premises of the form $\ulcorner\phi \Rightarrow (\psi \Rightarrow \theta)\urcorner$ and ϕ, and a conclusion of the form $\ulcorner \psi \Rightarrow \theta \urcorner$, where '$\Rightarrow$' stands for a conditionship relation discernible in the English indicative conditional which, allegedly, is intermediate in strength between strict implication and material implication (see ibid., p. 465). My view, however, is that, while it may be allowed that many English indicative conditionals require to be interpreted as involving a conditionship relation stronger than that of material implication (and which I shall continue to represent by '$\Rightarrow$'), in fact the first premise of McGee's example has the form $\ulcorner\phi \Rightarrow (\psi \supset \theta)\urcorner$—so that the embedded conditional is a *material* conditional—whereas the conclusion is indeed of the form $\ulcorner\psi \Rightarrow \theta\urcorner$. This being so, though, the failure of the conclusion to follow from the premises cannot be taken to impugn the validity of *modus ponens,* which is not exemplified by the inference in question; the only sort of fallacy involved in passing from these premises to this conclusion is purely one of equivocation.

My point may be made as follows. Plausibly—or so I would urge—McGee's first premise is just equivalent to

> If a Republican wins the election, then either it will be Reagan who wins or it will be Anderson.

Observe that from this and McGee's second premise *modus ponens* would have us infer

> Either it will be Reagan who wins or it will be Anderson,

which it *is* reasonable to believe in the circumstances described, because it is reasonable to believe a disjunction when it is reasonable to believe one of its disjuncts. Of course, this disjunction is just equivalent to the material conditional whose antecedent is

>   Reagan will not win the election

and whose consequent is

>   Anderson will win it.

Clearly, however, it is not this material conditional that is expressed in McGee's example by the *non*-embedded sentence

>   If it's not Reagan who wins, it will be Anderson

since we are invited to interpret this latter in a sense in which it expresses something *un*reasonable to believe in the circumstances described (unreasonable because of course in those circumstances it is reasonable to believe a conditional with the same antecedent but a contrary consequent). We should appreciate, however, that this very form of words *can* be interpreted in either of two ways: *either* as saying something of the form $\ulcorner \psi \Rightarrow \theta \urcorner$ (which interpretation is demanded of the non-embedded occurrence of the sentence in McGee's example), *or* as saying something of the form $\ulcorner \psi \supset \theta \urcorner$ —and that it is the latter interpretation which is demanded where the sentence in question appears embedded in McGee's first premise. If it is wondered why the latter interpretation is not readily available for the *non*-embedded conditional in McGee's example, the answer is familiar and straightforward enough: no conversational point is normally served by *asserting* something of the form $\ulcorner \psi \supset \theta \urcorner$ where ψ and θ are reasonably believed to be false, any more than it is by asserting something of the equivalent form $\ulcorner \sim \psi \vee \theta \urcorner$. This indeed is why, although in the circumstances of McGee's example it would be *reasonable to believe* the disjunction

> Either it will be Reagan who wins the election or it will be
> Anderson,

it would not be conversationally appropriate to *assert* this.

Perhaps it will be felt that I have not done enough to *prove* that McGee's first premise really is of the form $\ulcorner \phi \Rightarrow (\psi \supset \theta) \urcorner$. But it is enough that this is not a patently implausible interpretation, as I have attempted to show by pointing to the plausible equivalence of that premise with a sentence of the form $\ulcorner \phi \Rightarrow (\sim \psi \vee \theta) \urcorner$. The burden of proof lies rather with McGee to show that his first premise genuinely *is* of the form $\ulcorner \phi \Rightarrow (\psi \Rightarrow \theta) \urcorner$, since it is he who is relying on this assumption in order to challenge a deeply rooted principle of deductive inference. As things stand, it is more reasonable to appeal to the *validity* of *modus ponens* to show that McGee has misinterpreted the form of one of the sentences he invokes in his example. That is to say, a reasonable degree of logical conservatism entitles us to see in McGee's example not a breakdown of *modus ponens* but rather a demonstration that the English indicative conditional is sometimes interpretable as a material conditional and sometimes not—something which, as it happens, I have argued for elsewhere on quite independent grounds (see my 'Indicative and Counterfactual Conditionals', *Analysis* 39.3, June 1979, pp. 139–41). And, more generally, the lesson to be drawn is that logicians should be wary of jettisoning long-established principles of inference in response to the discovery of *apparent* counterexamples:

almost always it is safer to conclude that one's recalcitrant linguistic intuitions are erroneous or confused and to try to set them to rights by laying bare distinctions to which one was blind.

One final point. Even if it is granted that McGee's first premise *actually* has the form $\ulcorner \phi \Rightarrow (\psi \supset \theta \urcorner$, it might still be asked whether that very sentence could *also* be interpreted as expressing something of the form $\ulcorner \phi \Rightarrow (\psi \Rightarrow \theta) \urcorner$ and if so whether under such an interpretation it could be taken to express something reasonable to believe in the circumstances described in McGee's example. My answer is that I am far from sure that the kind of conditionship relation represented by '$\Rightarrow$' genuinely admits of this sort of embedding, but that to the limited extent that I can make sense of the suggestion that it does my reply to the second part of the question is 'No'. This is because the nearest I can come to allowing the sentence in question the proposed interpretation is to suppose that it might be understood as expressing in an elliptical way something that might more perspicuously be expressed by the following:

> If a Republican wins the election, then it will have been true to say that if it's not Reagan who wins, it will be Anderson.

And this, to the extent that I can make sense of it, expresses something which I consider it would have been *un*reasonable for those in the circumstances described in McGee's example to believe. (As may be gathered, one of the primary difficulties I see in the notion of embedding one '$\Rightarrow$' conditional within another in the way McGee envisages is the problem of accommodating their *tenses,* particularly where both conditionals are future tense ones: for straightforwardly embedding one such conditional within another as its consequent has the effect of transforming the tense of the embedded conditional from the future to the future future, so that the embedded conditional is not in fact equivalent to a non-embedded conditional of the same form—an effect which can only be overcome, and even then not entirely satisfactorily, by using the future perfect tense in the embedding conditional. But these are problems I cannot examine in detail here.)

9

Assumptions and the Supposed Counterexamples to Modus Ponens

D. E. Over

Is modus ponens a valid form of inference for the ordinary conditional? In a recent article Vann McGee has surprisingly argued 'no' on the basis of some very interesting examples. (See 'A Counterexample to Modus Ponens' in *The Journal of Philosophy,* September 1985, pp. 462–71.) I disagree with McGee's conclusion about modus ponens, but think that his examples should be used to make some important points about assumptions, beliefs, ordinary conditionals, and valid inference. These points will show that no real counterexamples to modus ponens have been given.

McGee presents a number of very closely related examples, and he describes (on p. 462) the first of these, which is also the most attractive, in the following way. (The numbering (1) – (3) has been added by me.)

Opinion polls taken just before the 1980 election showed the Republican Ronald Reagan decisively ahead of the Democrat Jimmy Carter, with the other Republican in the race, John Anderson, a distant third. Those apprised on the poll results believed, with good reason:

(1)   If a Republican wins the election, then if it's not Reagan who wins it will be Anderson.

(2)   A Republican will win.

Yet they did not have reason to believe

(3)   If it's not Reagan who wins, it will be Anderson.

McGee's conclusion in the light of examples of this type is that modus ponens is 'not strictly valid' (p. 462), and he expresses this point in the following way (p. 463):

> Sometimes the conclusion of an application of modus ponens is something we do not believe and should not believe, even though the premisses are propositions we believe very properly.

The first important point to notice is that McGee speaks of what we *believe* in the above quotation, and not of what we *assume*. In fact, he never speaks of modus ponens as the rule which allows us to infer a conclusion ψ from *assumptions* of the form ϕ and $\phi \Rightarrow \psi$ (or from assumptions these forms depend on), and yet this is how the rule is standardly stated in systems of natural deduction.[1] Actually (3) does validly follow given that we *assume* (1) and (2). Having a belief is not at all the same thing as making an assumption, and one respect in which they differ is that a belief *may* be suspended or set aside when an assumption by its very nature cannot be.

Suppose you believe that Reagan will win the election, and I ask you to consider what will happen if he does not win. You have no difficulty— you suspend or set to one side (in very informal terms) your belief about Reagan and certain other related beliefs, and then try to see what plausibly follows. But suppose now I ask you what will happen if Reagan does not win the election on the assumption that he will win it. This is puzzling because I am asking you, in effect, what follows from a contradiction. You do not immediately suspend or give up the assumption that Reagan will win the election, in order to decide what will happen if he does not win it, for what in that case would be the point of making the assumption? An assumption is a proposition we hang on to in circumstances like this, and to make the assumption is to agree for a time to hang on to the proposition.

Let us return to (3) above, and imagine that we are presented with this conditional on its own and asked whether we should believe it. To answer this question, we suppose that the antecedent of (3) is correct and, to avoid inconsistency, suspend some of our present beliefs, including, of course, our belief that Reagan will win the election. But by suspending that belief, we see that we no longer have any reason to believe (2) above, that a Republican will win (since we have presumably based this belief on our belief that Reagan will win). And as a result of these changes and what we know about the polls, we see that we should not believe (3), or more accurately the proposition which (3) expresses in this context.

The matter is very different in a context in which we infer (3) from the assumptions (1) and (2) by modus ponens. Here we cannot 'suspend' (2)—in this context (2) is an assumption, and the rule modus ponens does not permit us to discharge its assumptions (modus ponens is not like conditional introduction in this respect). And so (3) does follow given the assumption (1) and (2), or more accurately the proposition *here* expressed by (3) does follow from the propositions expressed by the assumptions (1) and (2).

There are in addition serious arguments against any attempt like McGee's to define validity in terms of justified belief. Of course, there is the well known point that the premisses of a valid argument may *individually* have a higher probability than its conclusion, and some would argue for the analogous point about justification.[2] Although the probability of ϕ may be relatively high and also the probability of ψ, the probability of ϕ & ψ may be relatively low. Admittedly, the probability of the conjunction of the premisses cannot be higher than that of the conclusion in a valid inference, but some epistemologists have argued that degree of justification is not similarly closed under known valid inference. They claim that one may not be justified in believing a proposition ψ, even though one is justified in believing the single proposition ϕ and knows that ψ may be validly inferred from ϕ.[3] This claim of these epistemologists should be questioned, I think, but should not be ruled out as trivially false by the very definition of validity. Finally, how would validity be defined for inferences in which assumptions were discharged? We would not want to be faced with McGee-type 'counterexamples' to disjunction elimination and existential elimination because assumptions had been discharged, leaving conclusions apparently unsupported by justified beliefs alone.

All the points made so far here are relevant to a much wider range of examples than those discussed by McGee, as illustrated by this inference:

(4)   If the polls are right, then Reagan must win;
(5)   The polls are right;
(6)   Reagan must win.

Suppose we ask whether we should believe (6) above when we merely have good reason to believe, but do not assume, (4) and (5). Surely (6) may strike us as too strong a statement to be worthy of belief in this kind of case. If (5) expresses only a reasonable belief, and not an assumption, then we may not hold it constant in the set of possible situations we use to determine the acceptability of what is here expressed by (6). To suspend our belief in (5) is to be prepared to consider possibilities in which Reagan does not win, and so these possibilities determine what is expressed by (6) and the un-acceptability of this proposition in this case. But if we go to a context in which we take (4) and (5) as assumptions, then we see that the relevant set of possible situations for judging the new use of (6) cannot have members in which either (4) or (5) is false. To assume (4) and (5) is to exclude such possibilities, and thus the 'narrower' proposition which (6) expresses in this context is true.

Some logicians would argue that there is a scope ambiguity in (4), and some of these would claim that (4) is only true (in the general circumstances described above) when it is given the logical form $\Box\,(\phi \Rightarrow \psi)$. With (4) in this form, of course, (4) – (6) would no longer appear to be an instance of modus ponens, and one would not need to ask whether (4) and (5) were assumptions. But this way of dealing with (4) – (6) as an apparent counterexample to modus ponens does not seem to be open to McGee, who appears to be committed to a hard line on giving logical forms to sentences in ordinary English. Towards the end of his paper he considers the claim that the logical form of (1) should be translated as $(\phi\,\&\,\psi) \Rightarrow \theta$ in a formal logic for the conditional. Clearly, if we only believed (1) in this form, then McGee could not argue that (1) – (3) is a counterexample to modus ponens. But he charges that it is unnatural to translate (1) in this way, and seems to take a hard line on translations in general in the following passage (p. 471):

> The selective use of unnatural translations is a powerful technique for improving the fit between the logic of natural language and the logic of a formal language. In fact, it is a little too powerful.

One suspects that, if only one is sly enough in giving translations, one can enable almost any logic to survive almost any counterexample. What is needed is a systematic account of how to give translations. In the absence of such an account, the unnatural translations will seem likely merely an ad hoc device for evading counterexamples.

McGee does have a good point, to some extent, about the practice of some logicians in trying to give such translations, but he himself is in serious trouble. His account of validity in terms of justified belief and his strong comments on translation imply the very implausible result that there are many types of quite straightforward counterexamples to modus ponens. And we can bring out even more clearly what is wrong with these supposed counterexamples by considering the following modification of (1) – (3):

(7)   If a Republican wins, then if he is not Reagan he will be Anderson;

(8)   A Republican will win;

(9)   If he is not Reagan, he will be Anderson.

The antecedent of (7) restricts the possibilities for the interpretation of the pronoun in its consequent. The second assumption (8) does the same job for the conclusion (9), and it would be a transparent mistake to try to interpret 'he' in some other way, in an attempt to show that (7) – (9) is invalid. McGee would make a mistake of this type if he thought of (8) as a relatively long-lasting mental state of justified belief outside of the context of this inference. He would not then see (8) as an assumption in an inference, determining in that context which proposition is expressed by (9).

An inference should be defined in terms of a relationship between assumptions and a conclusion, as is standard in logic. We should remember that the assumptions can restrict the relevant set of possibilities and so affect the propositions expressed under them, just as the antecedents can affect the propositions expressed by the consequents of conditionals. We must therefore be careful about the propositions expressed in inferences, particularly ones containing conditionals, if we wish to question their validity.[4] This is as true for (1) – (3) and (4) – (6) as it is for (7) – (9), and the point also applies to inferences of other forms, such as modus tollens, which can appear to have McGee-type 'counterexamples'. And when we use any of these valid inferences to extend our justified beliefs, we must be careful about which propositions we are to believe. Once these steps are taken, McGee-type 'counterexamples' to valid inference will disappear. Validity can be given a proper *semantic* definition in terms of propositions and truth preservation, and on that firm basis *epistemology* can legitimately ask the question of how justified belief is related to validity.[5]

NOTES

1. As McGee himself admits in a footnote (p. 462), modus ponens should really be seen as an inference involving *propositions* expressed by sentences of certain forms—a point relevant to what follows.

2. This criticism of McGee is stressed by Walter Sinnott-Armstrong, James Moor, and Robert Fogelin, 'A Defence of Modus Ponens,' *The Journal of Philosophy,* May 1986, pp. 296–300.

3. The influential source of this view seems to be Fred Dretske, 'Epistemic Operators,' *The Journal of Philosophy,* 1970, pp. 1007–23. It is closely related to the claim that knowledge is not closed under known logical implication—see also Robert Nozick, *Philosophical Explanations* (Harvard University Press, 1981), chap. 3.

4. This point can be used to support those who claim that (3) should not be interpreted in the same way as the consequent of (1). See, for example,

E. J. Lowe., 'Not a Counterexample to Modus Ponens,' *Analysis* 47.1, January 1987, pp. 44–7.

5. For helpful discussion, I should like to thank Simon Blackburn, Dorothy Edgington, Hugh Mellor, Richard Spencer-Smith, and especially Wilfred Hodges and E. J. Lowe. Very special thanks are due to Kit Fine, who must be ultimately responsible for any good ideas in the paper.

QUESTIONS

III. LOGIC AND INFERENCE

1. Following McGee, formulate your own counterexample to *modus ponens.*

2. Why does Over hold that deductive inference may not provide epistemic grounds for extending our beliefs?

3. According to Lowe, what is it to be a logical libertine?

IV

LOGIC AND FREEDOM

According to the law of excluded middle, all statements are either true, or if not true, then false. But consider the statement "Tomorrow you will call the White House." If the statement is true, then you are bound to make the call. If the statement is false, you are bound not to make the call. In either case only one possible course of action is open to you. So you are not free with regard to calling the White House tomorrow. And this argument applies to every one of your future actions. Thus you never act freely. Is this argument sound?

Gilbert Ryle thinks not, asserting that "events themselves cannot be made necessary by truths." Richard Taylor, however, argues that six presuppositions (including the law of excluded middle) widely accepted by contemporary philosophers imply the fatalistic conclusion that we have no more control over future events than we have now over past ones. Taylor and Steven M. Cahn offer a different argument leading to a fatalistic conclusion, claiming that we can only render true statements that are already true, and can only render false statements that are already false, and that even these conceptions make dubious sense.

10

'It Was To Be'

Gilbert Ryle

I want now to launch out without more ado into the full presentation and discussion of a concrete dilemma. It is a dilemma which, I expect, has occasionally bothered all of us, though, in its simplest form, not very often or for very long at a time. But it is intertwined with two other dilemmas, both of which probably have seriously worried nearly all of us. In its pure form it has not been seriously canvassed by any important Western philosopher, though the Stoics drew on it at certain points. It was, however, an ingredient in discussions of the theological doctrine of Predestination and I suspect that it has exerted a surreptitious influence on some of the champions and opponents of Determinism.

At a certain moment yesterday evening I coughed and at a certain moment yesterday evening I went to bed. It was therefore true on Saturday that on Sunday I would cough at the one moment and go to bed at the other. Indeed, it was true a thousand years ago that at certain moments on a certain Sunday a thousand years later I should cough and go to bed. But if it was true beforehand—forever beforehand—that I was to cough and go to bed at those two moments on Sunday, 25 January 1953, then it was impossible for me not to do so. There would be a contradiction in the joint assertion that it was true that I would do something at a certain time and that I did not do it. This argument is perfectly general. Whatever anyone ever does, whatever happens any-where to anything, could not *not* be done or happen, if it was true be-forehand that it was going to be done or was going to happen. So everything, including everything that we do, has been definitively booked from any earlier date you like to choose. Whatever is, was to be. So nothing that does occur could have been helped and nothing that has not actually been done could possibly have been done.

This point, that for whatever takes place it was antecedently true that it was going to take place, is sometimes picturesquely expressed by say-ing that the Book of Destiny has been written up in full from the begin-ning of time. A thing's actually taking place is, so to speak, merely the turning up of a passage that has for all time been written. This picture has led some fatalists to suppose that God, if there is one, or, we our-selves, if suitably favoured, may have access to this book and read ahead. But this is a fanciful embellishment upon what in itself is a severe and seemingly rigorous argument. We may call it 'the fatalist argument.'

Now the conclusion of this argument from antecedent truth, namely that nothing can be helped, goes directly counter to the piece of com-mon knowledge that some things are our own fault, that some threat-ening disasters can be foreseen and averted, and that there is plenty of room for precautions, planning and weighing alternatives. Even when we say nowadays of someone that he is born to be hanged or not born to be drowned, we say it as a humorous archaism. We really think that it depends very much on himself whether he is hanged or not, and that his chances of drowning are greater if he refuses to learn to swim. Yet even we are not altogether proof against the fatalist view of things. In a battle I may well come to the half-belief that either there exists some-where behind the enemy lines a bullet with my name on it, or there does not, so that taking cover is either of no avail or else unnecessary. In card-games and at the roulette-table it is easy to subside into the frame of mind of fancying that our fortunes are in some way pre-arranged, well though we know that it is silly to fancy this.

But how can we deny that whatever happens was booked to happen from all eternity? What is wrong with the argument from antecedent truth to the inevitability of what the antecedent truths are antecedently true about? For it certainly is logically impossible for a prophecy to be true and yet the event prophesied not to come about.

We should notice first of all that the premiss of the argument does not require that anyone, even God, *knows* any of these antecedent truths, or to put it picturesquely, that the Book of Destiny has been written by anybody or could be perused by anybody. This is just what distinguishes the pure fatalist argument from the mixed theological argument for pre-destination. This latter argument does turn on the supposition that God at least has foreknowledge of what is to take place, and perhaps also preordains it. But the pure fatalist argument turns only on the principle that it was true that a given thing would happen, before it did happen, i.e. that what is, was to be; not that it was known by anyone that it was to be. Yet even when we try hard to bear this point in mind, it is very easy inadvertently to reinterpret this initial principle into the supposi-tion that before the thing happened it was known by someone that it was booked to happen. For there is something intolerably vacuous in the idea of the eternal but unsupported pre-existence of truths in the fu-ture tense. When we say 'a thousand years ago it was true that I should now be saying what I am,' it is so difficult to give any body to this 'it' of which we say that it was then true, that we unwittingly fill it out with the familiar body of an expectation which someone once entertained, or of a piece of foreknowledge which someone once possessed. Yet to do this is to convert a principle which was worrying because, in a way, totally truistic, into a supposition which is unworrying because quasi-historical, entirely without evidence and most likely just false.

Very often, though certainly not always, when we say 'it was true
that . . .' or 'it is false that . . .' we are commenting on some actual pro-
nouncement made or opinion held by some identifiable person. Sometimes we are commenting in a more general way on a thing which some
people, unidentified and perhaps unidentifiable, have believed or now
believe. We can comment on the belief in the Evil Eye without being
able to name anyone who held it; we know that plenty of people did
hold it. Thus we can say 'it was true' or 'it is false' in passing verdicts
upon the pronouncements both of named and of nameless authors. But
in the premiss of the fatalist argument, namely that it was true before
something happened that it would happen, there is no implication of
anyone, named or unnamed, having made that prediction.

There remains a third thing that might be meant by 'it was true a
thousand years ago that a thousand years later these things would be
being said in this place,' namely that *if* anybody had made a prediction
to this effect, though doubtless nobody did, he would have been right.
It is not a case of an actual prediction having come true but of a conceivable prediction having come true. The event has not made an actual
prophecy come true. It has made a might-have-been prophecy come
true.

Or can we say even this? A target can be hit by an actual bullet, but
can it be hit by a might-have-been bullet? Or should we rather say only
that it could have been hit by a might-have-been bullet? The historical-
sounding phrases 'came true,' 'made true' and 'was fulfilled' apply well
enough to predictions actually made, but there is a detectable twist,
which may be an illegitimate twist, in saying that a might-have-been
prediction did come true or was made true by the event. If an unbacked
horse wins a race, we can say that it would have won money for its
backers, if only there had been any. But we cannot say that it did win
money for its backers, if only there had been any. There is no answer

to the question 'How much money did it win for them?' Correspondingly, we cannot with a clear conscience say of an event that it has fulfilled the predictions of it which could have been made, but only that
it would have fulfilled any predictions of it which might have been
made. There is no answer to the question 'Within what limits of preci-
sion were these might-have-been predictions correct about the time and
the loudness of my cough?'

Let us consider the notions of truth and falsity. In characterizing
somebody's statement, for example a statement in the future tense, as
true or as false, we usually though not always, mean to convey rather
more than that what was forecast did or did not take place. There is
something of a slur in 'false' and something honorific in 'true,' some
suggestion of the insincerity or sincerity of its author, or some suggestion of his rashness or cautiousness as an investigator. This is brought
out by our reluctance to characterize either as true or as false pure and
avowed guesses. If you make a guess at the winner of the race, it will
turn out right or wrong, correct or incorrect, but hardly true or false.
These epithets are inappropriate to avowed guesses, since the one epithet pays an extra tribute, the other conveys an extra adverse criticism
of the maker of the guess, neither of which can he merit. In guessing
there is no place for sincerity or insincerity, or for caution or rashness
in investigation. To make a guess is not to give an assurance and it is
not to declare the result of an investigation. Guessers are neither reliable
nor unreliable.

Doubtless we sometimes use 'true' without intending any connota-
tion of trustworthiness and, much less often, 'false' without any con-
notation of trust misplaced. But, for safety's sake, let us reword the
fatalist argument in terms of these thinner words, 'correct' and 'incorrect.' It would now run as follows. For any event that takes place, an
antecedent guess, if anyone had made one, that it was going to take

place, would have been correct, and an antecedent guess to the contrary, if anyone had made it, would have been incorrect. This formulation already sounds less alarming than the original formulation. The word 'guess' cuts out the covert threat of foreknowledge, or of there being budgets of antecedent forecasts, all meriting confidence before the event. What, now, of the notion of guesses in the future tense being correct or incorrect?

Antecedently to the running of most horse-races, some people guess that one horse will win, some that another will. Very often every horse has its backers. If, then, the race is run and won, then some of the backers will have guessed correctly and the rest will have guessed incorrectly. To say that someone's guess that Eclipse would win was correct is to say no more than that he guessed that Eclipse would win and Eclipse did win. But can we say in retrospect that his guess, which he made before the race, was already correct before the race? He made the correct guess two days ago, but was his guess correct during those two days? It certainly was not incorrect during those two days, but it does not follow, though it might seem to follow, that it was correct during those two days. Perhaps we feel unsure which we ought to say, whether that his guess was correct during those two days, though no one could know it to be so, or only that, as it turned out, it was during those two days going to prove correct, i.e. that the victory which did, in the event, make it correct had not yet happened. A prophecy is not fulfilled until the event forecast has happened. Just here is where 'correct' resembles 'fulfilled' and differs importantly from 'true.' The honorific connotations of 'true' can certainly attach to a person's forecasts from the moment at which they are made, so that if these forecasts turn out incorrect, while we withdraw the word 'true,' we do not necessarily withdraw the testimonials which it carried. The establishment of incorrectness certainly cancels 'true' but not, as a rule, so fiercely as to incline us to say 'false.'

The words 'true' and 'false' and the words 'correct' and 'incorrect' are adjectives, and this grammatical fact tempts us to suppose that trueness and falseness, correctness and incorrectness, and even, perhaps, fulfilledness and unfulfilledness must be qualities or properties resident in the propositions which they characterize. As sugar is sweet and white from the moment it comes into existence to the moment when it goes out of existence, so we are tempted to infer, by parity of reasoning, that the trueness or correctness of predictions and guesses must be features or properties which belong all the time to their possessors, whether we can detect their presence in them or not. But if we consider that 'deceased,' 'lamented' and 'extinct' are also adjectives, and yet certainly do not apply to people or mastodons while they exist, but only after they have ceased to exist, we may feel more cordial towards the idea that 'correct' is in a partly similar way a merely obituary and valedictory epithet, as 'fulfilled' more patently is. It is more like a verdict than a description. So when I tell you that if anyone had guessed that Eclipse would win today's race his guess would have turned out correct, I give you no more information about the past than is given by the evening newspaper which tells you that Eclipse won the race.

I want now to turn to the fatalist conclusion, namely that since whatever is was to be, therefore nothing can be helped. The argument seems to compel us to say that since the antecedent truth requires the event of which it is the true forecast, therefore this event is in some disastrous way fettered to or driven by or bequeathed by that antecedent truth— as if my coughing last night was made or obliged to occur by the antecedent truth that it was going to occur, perhaps in something like the way in which gunfire makes the windows rattle a moment or two after the discharge. What sort of necessity would this be?

To bring this out let us by way of contrast suppose that someone produced the strictly parallel argument, that for everything that happens, it is true for ever *afterwards* that it happened.

I coughed last night, so it is true today and will be true a thousand years hence that I coughed last night. But these posterior truths in the past tense, could not be true without my having coughed. Therefore my coughing was necessitated or obliged to have happened by the truth of these posterior chronicles of it. Clearly something which disturbed us in the original form of the argument is missing in this new form. We cheerfully grant that the occurrence of an event involves and is involved by the truth of subsequent records, actual or conceivable, to the effect that it occurred. For it does not even seem to render the occurrence a product or effect of these truths about it. On the contrary, in this case we are quite clear that it is the occurrence which makes the posterior truths about it true, not the posterior truths which make the occurrence occur. These posterior truths are shadows cast by the events, not the events shadows cast by these truths about them, since these belong to the posterity, not to the ancestry of the events.

Why does the fact that a posterior truth about an occurrence requires that occurrence not worry us in the way in which the fact that an anterior truth about an occurrence requires that occurrence does worry us? Why does the slogan 'Whatever is, always was to be' seem to imply that nothing can be helped, where the obverse slogan 'Whatever is, will always have been' does not seem to imply this? We are not exercised by the notorious fact that when the horse has already escaped it is too late to shut the stable door. We are sometimes exercised by the idea that as the horse is either going to escape or not going to escape, to shut the stable door beforehand is either unavailing or unnecessary. A large part of the reason is that in thinking of a predecessor making its successor necessary we unwittingly assimilate the necessitation to causal necessitation. Gunfire makes windows rattle a few seconds later, but rattling windows do not make gunfire happen a few seconds earlier, even though they may be perfect evidence that gunfire did happen a few seconds earlier. We slide, that is, into thinking of the anterior truths as *causes* of the happenings about which they were true, where the mere matter of their relative dates saves us from thinking of happenings as the effects of those truths about them which are posterior to them. Events cannot be the effects of their successors, any more than we can be the offspring of our posterity.

So let us look more suspiciously at the notions of *necessitating, making, obliging, requiring* and *involving* on which the argument turns. How is the notion of *requiring* or *involving* that we have been working with related to the notion of *causing*?

It is quite true that a backer cannot guess correctly that Eclipse will win without Eclipse winning and still it is quite false that his guessing made or caused Eclipse to win. To say that his guess that Eclipse would win was correct does logically involve or require that Eclipse won. To assert the one and deny the other would be to contradict oneself. To say that the backer guessed correctly is just to say that the horse which he guessed would win, did win. The one assertion cannot be true without the other assertion being true. But in this way in which one truth may require or involve another truth, an event cannot be one of the implications of a truth. Events can be effects, but they cannot be implications. Truths can be consequences of other truths, but they cannot be causes of effects or effects of causes.

In much the same way, the truth that someone revoked involves the truth that he had in his hand at least one card of the suit led. But he was not forced or coerced into having a card of that suit in his hand by the fact that he revoked. He could not both have revoked and not had a card of that suit in his hand, but this 'could not' does not connote any kind of duress. A proposition can imply another proposition, but it cannot thrust a card into a player's hand. The questions, what makes things happen, what prevents them from happening, and whether we can help

them or not, are entirely unaffected by the logical truism that a statement to the effect that something happens, is correct if and only if it
happens. Lots of things could have prevented Eclipse from winning the
race; lots of other things could have made his lead a longer one. But
one thing had no influence on the race at all, namely the fact that if anyone guessed that he would win, he guessed correctly.

We are now in a position to separate out one unquestionable and
very dull true proposition from another exciting but entirely false
proposition, both of which seem to be conveyed by the slogan 'What
is, always was to be.' It is an unquestionable and very dull truth that
for anything that happens, if anyone had at any previous time made the
guess that it would happen, his guess would have turned out correct.
The twin facts that the event could not take place without such a guess
turning out correct and that such a guess could not turn out correct without the event taking place tell us nothing whatsoever about how the
event was caused, whether it could have been prevented, or even
whether it could have been predicted with certainty or probability from
what had happened before. The menacing statement that what is was
to be, construed in one way, tells us only the trite truth that if it is true
to say (a) that something happened, then it is also true to say (b) that
that original statement (a) is true, no matter when this latter comment
(b) on the former statement (a) may be made.

The exciting but false proposition that the slogan seems to force
upon us is that whatever happens is inevitable or doomed, and, what
makes it sound even worse, *logically* inevitable or *logically* doomed—
somewhat as it is logically inevitable that the immediate successor of
any even number is an odd number. So what does 'inevitable' mean?
An avalanche may be, for all practical purposes, unavoidable. A mountaineer in the direct path of an avalanche can himself do nothing to stop
the avalanche or get himself out of its way, though a providential earth-

quake might conceivably divert the avalanche or a helicopter might conceivably lift him out of danger. His position is much worse, but only much worse, than that of a cyclist half a mile ahead of a lumbering steam-roller. It is extremely unlikely that the steam-roller will catch up with him at all, and even if it does so it is extremely likely that its driver will halt or that the cyclist himself will move off in good time. But these differences between the plights of the mountaineer and the cyclist are differences of degree only. The avalanche is practically unavoidable, but it is not logically inevitable. Only conclusions can be logically inevitable, given the premises, and an avalanche is not a conclusion. The fatalist doctrine, by contrast, is that everything is absolutely and logically inevitable in a way in which the avalanche is not absolutely or logically inevitable; that we are all absolutely and logically powerless where even the hapless mountaineer is only in a desperate plight and the cyclist is in no real danger at all; that everything is fettered by the Law of Contradiction to taking the course it does take, as odd numbers are bound to succeed even numbers. What sort of fetters are these purely logical fetters?

Certainly there are infinitely many cases of one truth making necessary the truth of another proposition. The truth that today is Monday makes necessary the truth of the proposition that tomorrow is Tuesday. It cannot be Monday today without tomorrow being Tuesday. A person who said 'It is Monday today but not Tuesday tomorrow' would be taking away with his left hand what he was giving with his right hand. But in the way in which some truths carry other truths with them or make them necessary, events themselves cannot be made necessary by truths. Things and events may be the topics of premises and conclusions, but they cannot themselves be premises or conclusions. You may preface a statement by the word 'therefore,' but you cannot pin either a 'therefore' or a 'perhaps not' on to a person or an avalanche. It is a partial parallel to say that while a sentence may contain or may be without a split infinitive, a road accident cannot either contain or lack a split infinitive, even though it is what a lot of sentences, with or without split infinitives in them, are about. It is true that an avalanche may be practically inescapable and the conclusion of an argument may be logically inescapable, but the avalanche has not got—nor does it lack—the inescapability of the conclusion of an argument. The fatalist theory tries to endue happenings with the inescapability of the conclusions of valid arguments. Our familiarity with the practical inescapability of some things, like some avalanches, helps us to yield to the view that really everything that happens is inescapable, only not now in the way in which some avalanches are inescapable and others not, but in the way in which logical consequences are inescapable, given their premises. The fatalist has tried to characterize happenings by predicates which are proper only to conclusions of arguments. He tried to flag my cough with a Q.E.D.

Before standing back to draw some morals from this dilemma between *whatever is was to be and some things which have happened could have been averted*, I want briefly to discuss one further point which may be of only domestic interest to professional philosophers. If a city-engineer has constructed a roundabout where there had been dangerous cross-roads, he may properly claim to have reduced the number of accidents. He may say that lots of accidents that would otherwise have occurred have been prevented by his piece of road improvement. But suppose we now ask him to give us a list of the particular accidents which he has averted. He can do nothing but laugh at us. If an accident has not happened, there is no 'it' to put down on a list of 'accidents prevented.' He can say that accidents of such and such kinds which used to be frequent are now rare. But he cannot say 'Yesterday's collision at midday between this fire-engine and that milk-float at this corner was, fortunately, averted.' There was no such collision, so he cannot say '*This* collision was averted.' To generalize this, we can never point to or name a particular happening and say of it 'This happening was averted,' and this logical truism seems to commit us to saying 'No happenings can be averted' and consequently 'it's no good trying to ensure or prevent anything happening.' So when we try to say that some things that happen could have been prevented; that some drownings, for example, would not have occurred had their victims learned to swim, we seem to be in a queer logical fix. We can say that a particular person would not have drowned had he been able to swim. But we cannot quite say that his lamented drowning would have been averted by swimming-lessons. For had he taken those lessons, he would not have drowned, and then we would not have had for a topic of discussion just that lamented drowning of which we want to say that *it* would have been prevented. We are left bereft of any 'it' at all. Averted fatalities are not fatalities. In short, we cannot, in logic, say of any designated fatality that it was averted—and this sounds like saying that it is logically impossible to avert any fatalities.

The situation is parallel to the following. If my parents had never met, I should not have been born, and had Napoleon known some things that he did not know the Battle of Waterloo would not have been fought. So we want to say that certain contingencies would have prevented me from being born and the Battle of Waterloo from being fought. But then there would have been no Gilbert Ryle and no Battle of Waterloo for historians to describe as not having been born and as not having been fought. What does not exist or happen cannot be named, individually indicated or put on a list, and cannot therefore be characterized as having been prevented from existing or happening. So though we are right to say that some sorts of accidents can be prevented, we cannot put this by saying that this designated accident might have been prevented from occurring—not because it was of an unpreventable sort, but because neither 'preventable' nor 'unpreventable' can be epithets of designated occurrences, any more than 'exists' or 'does not exist' can be predicated of designated things or persons. As 'unborn' cannot without absurdity be an epithet of a named person, so 'born' cannot without a queerly penetrating sort of redundancy be an epithet of him either. The question 'Were you born or not?' is, unless special insurance-policies are taken out, an unaskable question. Who could be asked it? Nor could one ask whether the Battle of Waterloo was fought or unfought. That it was fought goes with our having an *it* to talk about at all. There could not be a list of unfought battles, and a list of fought battles would contain just what a list of battles would contain. The question 'Could the Battle of Waterloo have been unfought?,' taken in one way, is an absurd question. Yet its absurdity is something quite different from the falsity that Napoleon's strategic decisions were forced upon him by the laws of logic.

I suspect that some of us have felt that the fatalist doctrine is unrefuted so long as no remedy has been found for the smell of logical trickiness that hangs about such arguments as 'Accidents can be prevented; therefore *this* accident could have been prevented' or 'I can bottle up my laughter; therefore I could have bottled up *that* hoot of laughter.' For it would not have been a hoot at all, and so not *that* hoot, had I bottled up my laughter. I could not, logically, have bottled *it* up. For *it* was an unbottled up hoot of laughter. The fact that it occurred is already contained in my allusion to 'that hoot of laughter.' So a sort of contradiction is produced when I try to say that that hoot of laughter need not have occurred. No such contradiction is produced when I say 'I did not have to hoot with laughter.' It is the demonstrative word '*that* . . .' which refused to consort with '. . . did not occur' or '. . . might not have occurred.'

This point seems to me to bring out an important difference between anterior truths and posterior truths, or between prophecies and chronicles. After 1815 there could be true and false statements mentioning the Battle of Waterloo in the past tense. After 1900 there could be true and false statements in the present and past tenses mentioning me. But before 1815 and 1900 there could not be true or false statements giving individual mention to the Battle of Waterloo or to me, and this not just because our names had not yet been given, nor yet just because no one happened to be well enough equipped to predict the future in very great detail, but for some more abstruse reason. The prediction of an event can, in principle, be as specific as you please. It does not matter if in fact no forecaster could know or reasonably believe his prediction to be true. If gifted with a lively imagination, he could freely concoct a story in the future tense with all sorts of minutiae in it and this elaborate story might happen to come true. But one thing he could not do—logically and not merely epistemologically could not do. He could not get the future events themselves for the heroes or heroines of his story, since while it is still an askable question whether or not a battle will be fought at Waterloo in 1815, he cannot use with their normal force the phrase 'the Battle of Waterloo' or the pronoun 'it.' While it is still an askable question whether my parents are going to have a fourth son, he cannot use as a name the name 'Gilbert Ryle' or use as a pronoun designating their fourth son the pronoun 'he.' Roughly, statements in the future tense cannot convey singular, but only general propositions, where statements in the present and past tense can convey both. More strictly, a statement to the effect that something will exist or happen is, in *so far*, a general statement. When I predict the next eclipse of the moon, I have indeed got the moon to make statements about, but I have not got her next eclipse to make statements about. Perhaps this is why novelists never write in the future tense, but only in the past tense. They could not get even the semblances of heroes or heroines into prophetic fiction, since the future tense of their would-be-prophetic mock-narratives would leave it open for their heroes and heroines not to be born. But as my phrase 'I have not got it to make statements about' stirs up a nest of logical hornets, I shall bid farewell for the present to this matter.

I have chosen to start with this particular dilemma for moderately sustained discussion for two or three connected reasons. But I did not do so for the reason that the issue is or ever has been of paramount importance in the Western world. No philosopher of the first or second rank has defended fatalism or been at great pains to attack it. Neither religion nor science wants it. Right-wing and Left-wing doctrines borrow nothing from it. On the other hand we do all have our fatalist moments; we do all know from inside what it is like to regard the course of events as the continuous unrolling of a scroll written from the beginning of time and admitting of no additions or amendments. Yet though we know what it is like to entertain this idea, still we are unimpassioned about it. We are not secret zealots for it or secret zealots against it. We are, nearly all of the time, though also aware that the argument for them is hard to rebut, cheerfully sure that the fatalist conclusions are false. The result is that we can study the issue in the spirit of critical playgoers, not that of electors whose votes are being solicited. It is not a burning issue. This is one reason why I have started with it.

Next, so little has the issue been debated by Western thinkers that I have been free to formulate for myself not only what seem to me the false steps in the fatalist argument from antecedent truth, but even that argument itself. I have not had to recapitulate a traditional controversy between philosophical schools, since there has been next to no such controversy, as there have, notoriously, existed protracted controversies about Predestination and Determinism. You know, from inside your own skins, all that needs to be known about the issue. There are no cards of erudition up my sleeve.

Thirdly, the issue is in a way a very simple one, a very important one and an illuminatingly tricky one. It is simple in that so few pivot-concepts are involved—just, in the first instance, the untechnical concepts of *event, before* and *after, truth, necessity, cause, prevention, fault* and *responsibility*—and of course we all know our ways about in them—or do we? They are public highway concepts, not craftsmen's concepts; so none of us can get lost in them—or can we? It is important in that if the fatalist conclusion were true, then nearly the whole of our normal religious, moral, political, historical, scientific and pedagogic thinking would be on entirely the wrong lines. We cannot shape the world of tomorrow, since it has already been shaped once and for all. It is a tricky issue because there is not any regulation or argumentative manoeuvre by which it can be settled. I have produced quite an apparatus of somewhat elaborate arguments, all of which need expansion and reinforcement. I expect that the logical ice is pretty thin under some of them. It would not trouble me if the ice broke, since the stamp of the foot which broke it would itself be a partially decisive move. But even this move would not be the playing of any regulation logical manoeuvre. Such regulation manoeuvres exist only for dead philosophical issues. It was their death which promoted the decisive moves up to the status of regulation manoeuvres.

Now for some general morals which can be drawn from the existence of this dilemma and from attempts to resolve it. It arose out of two seemingly innocent and unquestionable propositions, propositions which are so well embedded in what I may vaguely call 'common knowledge' that we should hardly wish to give them the grand title of 'theories.' These two propositions were, first, that some statements in the future tense are or come true, and, second, that we often can and

sometimes should secure that certain things do happen and that certain
other things do not happen. Neither of these innocent-seeming propositions is as yet a philosopher's speculation, or even a scientist's hypothesis or a theologian's doctrine. They are just platitudes. We should,
however, notice that it would not very often occur to anyone to state
these platitudes. People say of this particular prediction that it was fulfilled and of that particular guess that it turned out correct. To say that
some statements in the future tense are true is a generalization of these
particular concrete comments. But it is a generalization which there is
not usually any point in propounding. Similarly people say of particular
offences that they ought not to have been committed and of particular
catastrophes that they could or could not have been prevented. It is relatively rare to stand back and say in general terms that people sometimes do wrong and that mishaps are sometimes our own fault. None
the less, there are occasions, long before philosophical or scientific
speculations begin, on which people do deliver generalities of these
sorts. It is part of the business of the teacher and the preacher, of the
judge and the doctor, of Solon and Æsop, to say general things, with
concrete examples of which everyone is entirely familiar. In one way
the generality is not and cannot be news to anyone that every day has
its yesterday and every day has its tomorrow; and yet, in another way,
this can be a sort of news. There was the first occasion on which this
generality was presented to us, and very surprising it was—despite the
fact that on every day since infancy we had thought about its particular
yesterday and its particular tomorrow. There is, anyhow at the start, an
important sort of unfamiliarity about such generalizations of the totally
familiar. We do not yet know how we should and how we should not
operate with them, although we know quite well how to operate with
the daily particularities of which they are the generalizations. We make
no foot-faults on Monday morning with 'will be' and 'was'; but when

required to deal in the general case with the notions of *the future* and *the past*, we are no longer sure of our feet.

The two platitudes from which the trouble arose are not in direct conflict with one another. It is real or seeming deductions from the one which quarrel with the other, or else with real or seeming deductions from it. They are not rivals such that before these deductions had been noticed anyone would want to say 'I accept the proposition that some statements in the future tense are fulfilled, so naturally I reject the proposition that some things need not and should not have happened.' It is because the former proposition seems indirectly to entail that what is was from all eternity going to be and because this, in its turn, seems to entail that nothing is anybody's fault, that some thinkers have felt forced to make a choice between the two platitudes. Aristotle, for example, rejected, with reservations, the platitude that statements in the future tense are true or false. Certain Stoics rejected the platitude that we are responsible for some things that happen. If we accept both platitudes, it is because we think that the fatalist deductions from 'it was true . . .' are fallacious or else that certain deductions drawn from 'some things are our fault' are fallacious, or both.

But this raises a thorny general question. How is it that in their most concrete, ground-floor employment, concepts like *will be, was, correct, must, make, prevent* and *fault* behave, in the main, with exemplary docility, but become wild when employed in what are mere first-floor generalizations of their ground-floor employments? We are in very little danger of giving or taking the wrong logical change in our daily marketing uses of 'tomorrow' and 'yesterday.' We know perfectly well how to make our daily sales and purchases with them. Yet in the general case, when we try to negotiate with 'what is,' 'what is to be,' 'what was' and 'what was to be' we very easily get our accounts in a muddle. We are quite at home with 'therefore' and all at sea with 'necessary.'

How is it that we get our accounts in a muddle when we try to do wholesale business with ideas with which in retail trade we operate quite efficiently every day of our lives? Later on I hope to give something of an answer to this question. For the moment I merely advertise it.

Meanwhile there is another feature of the issue to which we should attend. I have indicated that the quandary, though relatively simple, does depend upon a smallish number of concepts, namely, in the first instance, upon those of *event, before* and *after, truth, necessity, cause, prevention, fault* and *responsibility*. Now there is not just one of these concepts which is the logical trouble-maker. The trouble arises out of the interplay between all of them. The litigation between the two initial platitudes involves a whole web of conflicting interests. There is not just a single recalcitrant knot in the middle of one of the concepts involved. All the strings between all of them are implicated in the one tangle.

I mention this point because some people have got the idea from some of the professions though not, I think, the practices of philosophers, that doing philosophy consists or should consist of untying logical knots one at a time—as if, to burlesque the idea, it would have been quite proper and feasible for Hume on Monday to analyse the use of the term 'cause,' and then on Tuesday, Wednesday and Thursday to move on to analyse *seriatim* the uses of the terms 'causeway,' 'cautery' and 'caution,' in alphabetical order.

I have no special objection to or any special liking for the fashion of describing as 'analysis' the sort or sorts of conceptual examination which constitute philosophizing. But the idea is totally false that this examination is a sort of garage inspection of one conceptual vehicle at a time. On the contrary, to put it dogmatically, it is always a traffic-inspector's examination of a conceptual traffic-block, involving at least two streams of vehicles hailing from the theories, or points of view or platitudes which are at cross-purposes with one another.

One other point arises in connexion with this last one. The child can be taught a lot of words, one after another; or, when consulting the dictionary to find out the meanings of some unfamiliar words in a difficult passage, he can look up these words separately in alphabetical or any other order. This fact, among others, has encouraged the notion that the ideas or concepts conveyed by these words are something like separately movable and examinable chessmen, coins, counters, snapshots— or words. But we should not think of what a word conveys as if it were, like the word, a sort of counter, though unlike the word, an invisible counter. Consider a wicket-keeper. He is an individual, who can be fetched out of the team and separately interviewed, photographed or massaged. But his role in the game, namely the wicket-keeping that he does, so interlocks with what the other cricketers do, that if they stopped playing, he could not go on keeping wicket. He alone performs his particular role, yet he cannot perform it alone. For him to keep wicket, there must be a wicket, a pitch, a ball, a bat, a bowler and a batsman. Even that is not enough. There must be a game in progress and not, for example, a funeral, a fight or a dance; and the game must be a game of cricket and not, for example, a game of 'Touch Last.' The same man who keeps wicket on Saturday may play tennis on Sunday. But he cannot keep wicket in a game of tennis. He can switch from one set of sporting functions to another, but one of his functions cannot be switched to the other game. In much the same way, concepts are not things, as words are, but rather the functionings of words, as keeping wicket is the functioning of the wicket-keeper. Very much as the functioning of the wicket-keeper interlocks with the functioning of the bowler, the batsman and the rest, so the functioning of a word interlocks with the functioning of the other members of the team for which that word is playing. One word may have two or more functions; but one of its functions cannot change places with another.

Let me illustrate. A game like Bridge or Poker has a fairly elaborate and well-organized technical vocabulary, as in different degrees have nearly all games, crafts, professions, hobbies and sciences. Naturally the technical terms peculiar to Bridge have to be learned. How do we learn them? One thing is clear. We do not and could not master the use of one of them without yet having begun to learn the use of any of the others. It would be absurd to try to teach a boy how to use the concept of *cross-ruff*, without yet having introduced him to the notions of *following suit, trump* and *partner*. But if he has been introduced to the way these terms function together in Bridge talk, then he has begun to learn some of the elements of Bridge. Or consider the technical dictions of English lawyers. Could a student claim to understand one or seven of its specialist terms, though knowing nothing of the law? or claim to know the law while not understanding at least a considerable fraction of its terminological apparatus? The terminological apparatus of a science is in the same way a team and not a mere mob of terms. The part played by one of them belongs, with the parts played by the others, to the particular game or work of the whole apparatus. A person who had merely memorized the dictionary-paraphrases of a thousand technical terms of physics or economics would not yet have begun to be a physicist or an economist. He would not yet have learned how to operate with those terms. So he would not yet understand them. If he cannot yet think any of the thoughts of economic theory, he has not yet got any of its special concepts.

What is true of the more or less highly technical terms of games, the law, the sciences, the trades and professions is true also, with important modifications, of the terms of everyday discourse. These stand to the terms of the specialists very much as civilians stand to the officers, non-commissioned officers and private soldiers of different units in the Army. The rights, duties and privileges of soldiers are carefully prescribed; their uniforms, badges, stripes and buttons show their ranks, trades and units; drill, discipline and daily orders mould their movements. But civilians too have their codes, their habits, and their etiquettes; their work, pay and taxes tend to be regular; their social circles, their apparel and their amusements, though not regimented, are pretty stable. We know, too, how in this twentieth century of ours the distinctions between civilians and soldiers are notoriously blurred. Similarly the line between un-technical and technical dictions is a blurred line, and one frequently crossed in both directions; and though untechnical terms have not got their functions officially imposed upon them, they have their functions, privileges and immunities none the less. They resemble civilians rather than soldiers, but most of them also resemble rate-payers rather than gipsies.

The functions of technical terms, that is, the concepts conveyed by them, are more or less severely regimented. The kinds of interplay of function for which they are built are relatively definite and circumscribed. Yet untechnical terms, too, though they belong to no single organized unit, still have their individual places in indefinitely many overlapping and intermingling *milieus*.

It can be appreciated, consequently, that the functions of terms become both narrower and better prescribed as they become more official. Their roles in discourse can be more strictly formulated as their commitments are reduced in number and in scope. Hence, the more exactly their duties come to being fixed by charters and commissions, the further they move from being philosophically interesting. The official concepts of Bridge generate few if any logical puzzles. Disputes could not be settled or rubbers won if they were generated. Logical puzzles arise especially over concepts that are uncommissioned, namely the civilian concepts which, instead of having been conscripted and trained for just one definite and appointed niche in one organized unit, have grown up into their special but unappointed places in a thousand unchartered groups and informal associations. This is why an issue like the fatalist issue, though starting with a quite slender stem, ramifies out so swiftly into seemingly remote sectors of human interests. The question whether statements in the future tense can be true swiftly opened out into, among a thousand others, the question whether anything is gained by learning to swim.

Certain thinkers, properly impressed by the excellent logical discipline of the technical concepts of long-established and well consolidated sciences like pure mathematics and mechanics, have urged that intellectual progress is impeded by the survival of the unofficial concepts of unspecialized thought; as if there were something damagingly amateurish or infantile in the businesses and avocations of unconscripted civilians. Members of the Portland Club, the M.C.C., or the Law Faculty of a University might, with even greater justice, contrast their own scrupulously pruned and even carpentered terms of art with the undesigned dictions of everyday discourse. It is, of course, quite true that scientific, legal or financial thinking could not be conducted only in colloquial idioms. But it is quite false that people could, even in Utopia, be given their first lessons in talking and thinking in the terms of this or that technical apparatus. Fingers and feet are, for many special purposes, grossly inefficient instruments. But to replace the infant's fingers and feet by pliers and pedals would not be a good plan—especially as the employment of pliers and pedals themselves depends upon the employment of fingers and feet. Nor does the specialist when he comes to use the designed terms of his art cease to depend upon the concepts which he began to master in the nursery, any more than the driver, whose skill and interests are concentrated on the mechanically complex and delicate works of his car, cease to avail himself of the mechanically crude properties of the public highway. He could not use his car without using the roads, though he could, as the pedestrian that he often is, use these same roads without using his car.

11

Fatalism

Richard Taylor

A fatalist—if there is any such—thinks he cannot do anything about the future. He thinks it is not up to him what is going to happen next year, tomorrow, or the very next moment. He thinks that even his own behavior is not in the least within his power, any more than the motions of the heavenly bodies, the events of remote history, or the political developments in China. It would, accordingly, be pointless for him to deliberate about what he is going to do, for a man deliberates only about such things as he believes are within his power to do and to forego, or to affect by his doings and foregoings.

A fatalist, in short, thinks of the future in the manner in which we all think of the past. For we do all believe that it is not up to us what happened last year, yesterday, or even a moment ago, that these things are not within our power, any more than are the motions of the heavens, the events of remote history or of China. And we are not, in fact, ever tempted to deliberate about what we have done and left undone. At best we can speculate about these things, rejoice over them or repent, draw conclusions from such evidence as we have, or perhaps—if we are not fatalists about the future—extract lessons and precepts to apply henceforth. As for what has in fact happened, we must simply take it as given; the possibilities for action, if there are any, do not lie there. We may, indeed, say that some of those past things *were* once within our power, while they were still future—but this expresses our attitude toward the future, not the past.

There are various ways in which a man might get to thinking in this fatalistic way about the future, but they would be most likely to result from ideas derived from theology or physics. Thus, if God is really all-knowing and all-powerful, then, one might suppose, perhaps he has already arranged for everything to happen just as it is going to happen, and there is nothing left for you or me to do about it. Or, without bringing God into the picture, one might suppose that everything happens in accordance with invariable laws, that whatever happens in the world at any future time is the only thing that can then happen, given that certain other things were happening just before, and that these, in turn, are the only things that can happen at that time, given the total state of the world just before then, and so on, so that again, there is nothing left for us to do about it. True, what we do in the meantime will be a factor in determining how some things finally turn out—but these things that we are *going* to do will perhaps be only the causal consequences of what will be going on just before we do them, and so on back to a not distant point at which it seems obvious that we have nothing to do with what happens then. Many philosophers, particularly in the seventeenth and eighteenth centuries, have found this line of thought quite compelling.

I want to show that certain presuppositions made almost universally in contemporary philosophy yield a proof that fatalism is true, without any recourse to theology or physics. If, to be sure, it is assumed that there is an omniscient god, then that assumption can be worked into the argument so as to convey the reasoning more easily to the unphilosophical imagination, but this assumption would add nothing to the force of the argument, and will therefore be omitted here. And similarly, certain views about natural laws could be appended to the argument, perhaps for similar purposes, but they, too, would add nothing to its validity, and will therefore be ignored.

Presuppositions. The only presuppositions we shall need are the six following.

First, we presuppose that any proposition whatever is either true or, if not true, then false. This is simply the standard interpretation, *tertium non datur,* of the law of excluded middle, usually symbolized (p v -p), which is generally admitted to be a necessary truth.

Second, we presuppose that, if any state of affairs is sufficient for, though logically unrelated to, the occurence of some further condition at the same or any other time, then the former cannot occur without the latter occuring also. This is simply the standard manner in which the concept of *sufficiency* is explicated. Another and perhaps better way of saying the same thing is that, if one state of affairs *ensures* without logically entailing the occurrence of another, then the former cannot occur without the latter occuring. Ingestion of cyanide, for instance, *ensures* death under certain familar circumstances, though the two states of affairs are not logically related.

Third, we presuppose that, if the occurrence of any condition is necessary for, but logically unrelated to, the occurrence of some other condition at the same or any other time, then the latter cannot occur without the former occurring also. This is simply the standard manner in which the concept of a *necessary condition* is explicated. Another and perhaps better way of saying the same thing is that, if one state of affairs is *essential* for another, then the latter cannot occur without it. Oxygen, for instance, is *essential to* (though it does not by itself ensure) the maintenance of human life—though it is not logically impossible that we should live without it.

Fourth, we presuppose that, if one condition or set of conditions is sufficient for (ensures) another, then that other is necessary (essential) for it, and conversely, if one condition or set of conditions is necessary (essential) for another, then that other is sufficient for (ensures) it. This is but a logical consequence of the second and third presuppositions.

Fifth, we presuppose that no agent can perform any given act if there is lacking, at the same or any other time, some condition necessary for the occurrence of that act. This follows, simply from the idea of anything being essential for the accomplishment of something else. I cannot, for example, live without oxygen, or swim five miles without ever having been in water, or read a given page of print without having learned Russian, or win a certain election without having been nominated, and so on.

And *sixth,* we presuppose that time is not by itself "efficacious"; that is, that the mere passage of time does not augment or diminish the capacities of anything and, in particular, that it does not enhance or decrease an agent's powers or abilities. This means that if any substance or agent gains or loses powers or abilities over the course of time— such as, for instance, the power of a substance to corrode, or a man to do thirty push-ups, and so on—then such gain or loss is always the result of something other than the mere passage of time.

With these presuppositions before us, we now consider two situations in turn, the relations involved in each of them being identical except for certain temporal ones.

The first situation. We imagine that I am about to open my morning newspaper to glance over the headlines. We assume, further, that conditions are such that only if there was a naval battle yesterday does the newspaper carry a certain kind (shape) of headline—i.e., that such a battle is essential for this kind of headline—whereas if it carries a certain different sort (shape) of headline, this will ensure that there was no such battle. Now, then, I am about to perform one or the other of two acts, namely, one of seeing a headline of the first kind, or one of seeing a headline of the second kind. Call these alternative acts S and S' respectively. And call the propositions, "A naval battle occurred yesterday" and "No naval battle occurred yesterday", P and P' respectively. We can assert, then, that if I perform act S', then my doing such will ensure that there was a naval battle yesterday (i.e., that P is true), whereas if I perform S', then my doing that will ensure that no such battle occurred (or, that P' is true).

With reference to this situation, then, let us now ask whether it is up to me which sort of headline I shall read as I open the newspaper; that is, let us see whether the following proposition is true:

(A)   It is within my power to do S, and it is also within my power to do S'.

It seems quite obvious that this is not true. For if both these acts were equally within my power, that is, if it were up to me which one to do, then it would also be up to me whether or not a naval battle has taken place, giving me a power over the past which I plainly do not possess. It will be well, however, to express this point in the form of a proof, as follows:

1. If P is true, then it is not within my power to do S' (for in case P is true, then there is, or was, lacking a condition essential for my doing S', the condition, namely, of there being no naval battle yesterday).
2. But if P' is true, then it is not within my power to do S (for a similar reason).
3. But either P is true, or P' is true.
∴ 4. Either it is not within my power to do S, or it is not within my power to do S';

and (A) is accordingly false. A common-sense way of expressing this is to say that what sort of headline I see depends, among other things, on whether a naval battle took place yesterday, and that, in turn, is not up to me.

Now this conclusion is perfectly in accordance with common sense, for we all are, as noted, fatalists with respect to the past. No one considers past events as being within his power to control; we simply have to take them as they have happened and make the best of them. It is significant to note, however, that, in the hypothetical sense in which statements of human power or ability are usually formulated, one *does* have power over the past. For we can surely assert that, *if* I do S, this will ensure that a naval battle occurred yesterday, whereas *if* alternatively, I do S', this will equally ensure the nonoccurrence of such a battle, since these acts are, in terms of our example, quite sufficient for the truth of P and P' respectively. Or we can equally say that I can ensure the occurrence of such a battle yesterday simply by doing S and that I can ensure its nonoccurrence simply by doing S'. Indeed, if I should ask *how* I can go about ensuring that no naval battle occurred yesterday, perfectly straightforward instructions can be given, namely, the instruction to do S' and by all means to avoid doing S. But of course the hitch is that I cannot do S' *unless* P' is true, the occurrence of the battle in question rendering me quite powerless to do it.

The second situation. Let us now imagine that I am a naval commander, about to issue my order of the day to the fleet. We assume, further, that, within the totality of other conditions prevailing, my issuing of a certain kind of order will ensure that a naval battle will occur tomorrow, whereas if I issue another kind of order, this will ensure that no naval battle occurs. Now, then, I am about to perform one or the other of these two acts, namely, one of issuing an order of the first sort or one of the second sort. Call these alternative acts O and O' respectively. And call the two propositions, "A naval battle will occur tomorrow" and "No naval battle will occur tomorrow," Q and Q' respectively. We can assert, then, that, if I do act O, then my doing such will ensure that there will be a naval battle, whereas if I do O', my doing that will ensure that no naval battle will occur.

With reference to this situation, then, let us now ask whether it is up to me which sort of order I issue; that is, let us see whether the following proposition is true:

(B) It is within my power to do O, and it is also within my power to do O'.

Anyone, except a fatalist, would be inclined to say that, in the situation we have envisaged, this proposition might well be true, that is, that both acts are quite within my power (granting that I cannot do both at once). For in the circumstances we assume to prevail, it is, one would think, up to me as the commander whether the naval battle occurs or not; it depends only on what kind of order I issue, given all the other conditions as they are, and what kind of order is issued is something quite within my power. It is precisely the denial that such propositions are ever true that would render one a fatalist.

But we have, unfortunately, the same formal argument to show that (B) is false that we had for proving the falsity of (A), namely:

1'. If Q is true, then it is not within my power to do O' (for in case Q is true, then there is, or will be, lacking a condition essential for my doing O', the condition, namely, of there being no naval battle tomorrow).

2'. But if Q' is true, then it is not within my power to do O (for a similar reason).

3'.   But either Q is true, or Q' is true.

∴ 4'.   Either it is not within my power to do O, or it is not within my power to do O';

and (B) is accordingly false. Another way of expressing this is to say that what sort of order I issue depends, among other things, on whether a naval battle takes place tomorrow—for in this situation a naval battle tomorrow is (by our fourth presupposition) a necessary condition of my doing O, whereas no naval battle tomorrow is equally essential for my doing O'.

Considerations of time. Here it might be tempting, at first, to say that *time* makes a difference, and that no condition can be necessary for any other *before* that condition exists. But this escape is closed by both our fifth and sixth presuppositions. Surely if some condition, at *any* given time, whether past, present, or future, is necessary for the occurrence of something else, and that condition does not in fact exist *at the time it is needed,* then nothing we do can be of any avail in bringing about that occurrence for which it is necessary. To deny this would be equivalent to saying that I can do something now which is, together with other conditions prevailing, sufficient for, or which ensures, the occurrence of something else in the future, *without* getting that future occurrence as a result. This is absurd in itself and contrary to our second presupposition. And if one should suggest, in spite of all this, that a state of affairs that exists *not yet* cannot, just because of this temporal removal, be a necessary condition of *anything* existing prior to it, this would be logically equivalent to saying that no present state of affairs can ensure another subsequent to it. We could with equal justice say that a state of affairs, such as yesterday's naval battle, which exists *no longer,* cannot be a necessary condition of anything existing subsequently, there being the same temporal interval here; and this would be arbitrary and false. All that is needed, to restrict the powers that I imagine myself to have to do this or that, is that some condition essential to my doing it *does* not, *did* not, or *will* not occur.

Nor can we wriggle out of fatalism by representing this sort of situation as one in which there is a simple loss of ability or power resulting from the passage of time. For according to our sixth presupposition, the mere passage of time does not enhance or diminish the powers or abilities of anything. We cannot, therefore, say that I have the power to do *O'* until, say, tomorrow's naval battle occurs, or the power to do *O* until tomorrow arrives and we find no naval battle occurring, and so on. What restricts the range of my power to do this thing or that is not the mere *temporal* relations between my acts and certain other states of affairs, but the very existence of those states of affairs themselves; and according to our first presupposition, the fact of tomorrow's containing, or lacking, a naval battle, as the case may be, is no less a fact than yesterday's containing or lacking one. If, at any time, I lack the power to perform a certain act, then it can only be the result of something, other than the passage of time, that has happened, is happening, or will happen. The fact that there *is going* to be a naval battle tomorrow is quite enough to render me unable to do *O'*, just as the fact that there *has been* a naval battle yesterday renders me unable to do *S'*, the nonoccurrence of those conditions being essential, respectively, for my doing those things.

Causation. Again, it does no good here to appeal to any particular analyses of causation, or to the fact, if it is one, that causes only "work" forwards and not backwards, for our problem has been formulated without any reference to causation. It may be, for all we know, that causal relations have an unalterable direction (which is an unclear claim in itself), but it is very certain that the relations of necessity and sufficiency between events or states of affairs have not, and it is in terms of these that our data have been described.

The law of excluded middle. There is, of course, one other way to avoid fatalism, and that is to deny one of the premises used to refute (*B*). The first two, hypothetical, premises cannot be denied, however, without our having to reject all but the first, and perhaps the last, of our original six presuppositions, and none of these seems the least doubtful. And the third premise—that either *Q* is true, or *Q′* is true—can be denied only by rejecting the first of our six presuppositions, that is, by rejecting the standard interpretation, *tertium non datur,* of what is called the law of excluded middle.

This last escape has, however, been attempted, and it apparently involves no absurdity. Aristotle, according to an interpretation that is sometimes rendered of his *De Interpretation,* rejected it. According to this view, the disjunction (*Q* v *Q′*) or, equivalently, (*Q* v −*Q*), which is an instance of the law in question, is a necessary truth. Neither of its disjuncts, however—i.e., neither *Q*, nor *Q′*—is a necessary truth nor, indeed, even a truth, but is instead a mere "possibility," or "contingency" (whatever that may mean). And there is, it would seem, no obvious absurdity in supposing that two propositions, neither of them true and neither of them false, but each "possible," might nevertheless combine into a disjunction which is a necessary truth—for that disjunction might, as this one plainly does, exhaust the possibilities.

Indeed, by assuming the truth of (*B*)—i.e., the statement that it is within my power to do *O* and it is also within my power to do *O′*—and substituting this as our third premise, a formal argument can be rendered to prove that a disjunction of contradictories might disjoin propositions which are neither true nor false. Thus:

1″.   If *Q* is true, then it is not within my power to do *O′*.
2″.   But if *Q′* is true, then it is not within my power to do *O*.

3".   But it is within my power to do O, and it is also within my power to do O'.

∴ 4". Q' is not true, and Q is not true;

and to this we can add that, since Q and Q' are logical contradictories, such that if either is false then the other is true, then Q is not false, and Q' is not false—i.e., that neither of them is true and neither of them false.

There seems to be no good argument against this line of thought which does not presuppose the very thing at issue, that is, which does not presuppose, not just the truth of a disjunction of contradictories, which is here preserved, but one special interpretation of the law thus expressed, namely, that no third value, like "possible," can ever be assigned to any proposition. And that particular interpretation can, perhaps, be regarded as a more or less arbitrary restriction.

We would not, furthermore, be obliged by this line of thought to reject the traditional interpretation of the so-called law of contradiction, which can be expressed by saying that, concerning any proposition, not both it and its contradictory can be true—which is clearly consistent with what is here suggested.

Nor need we suppose that, from a sense of neatness and consistency, we ought to apply the same considerations to our first situation and to proposition (A)—that, if we so interpret the law in question as to avoid fatalism with respect to the future, then we ought to retain the same interpretation as it applies to things past. The difference here is that we have not the slightest inclination to suppose that it is at all within our power what happened in the past, or that propositions like (A) in situations such as we have described are ever true, whereas we do, if we are not fatalists, believe that it is sometimes within our power what happens in the future, that is, that propositions like (*B*) are sometimes true. And it was only from the desire to perserve the truth of (*B*), but not (*A*), and thus avoid fatalism, that the *tertium non datur* was doubted, using (*B*) as a premise.

Temporal efficacy. It now becomes apparent, however, that if we seek to avoid fatalism by this device, then we shall have to reject not only our first but also our sixth presupposition; for on this view time will by itself have the power to render true or false certain propositions which were hitherto neither, and this is an "efficacy" of sorts. In fact, it is doubtful whether one can in any way avoid fatalism with respect to the future while conceding that things past are, by virtue of their pastness alone, no longer within our power without also conceding an efficacy to time; for *any* such view will entail that future possibilities, at one time within our power to realize or not, cease to be such *merely* as a result of the passage of time—which is precisely what our sixth presupposition denies. Indeed, this is probably the whole point in casting doubt upon the law of excluded middle in the first place, namely, to call attention to the status of some future things as mere possibilities, thus denying both their complete factuality and their complete lack of it. If so, then our first and sixth presuppositions are inseparably linked, standing or falling together.

The assertion of fatalism. Of course one other possibility remains, and that is to assert, out of a respect for the law of excluded middle and a preference for viewing things under the aspect of eternity, that fatalism is indeed a true doctrine, that propositions such as (*B*) are, like (*A*), never true in such situations as we have described, and that the difference in our *attitudes* toward things future and past, which leads us to call some of the former but none of the latter "possibilities," results entirely from epistemological and psychological considerations—such as, that we happen to *know* more about what the past contains than about what is contained in the future, that our memory extends to past experiences rather than future ones, and so on. Apart from subjective feelings of our power to control things, there seem to be no good philosophical reasons against this opinion, and very strong ones in its favor.

Time, Truth, and Ability

Richard Taylor and Steven M. Cahn

We shall here be concerned with statements of the form '*M* does *A* at *t*,' wherein *M* designates a specific person, *A* a specific action and *t* a specific time. We shall refer to these as R-statements. Thus, 'Someone raised his hand at noon last Tuesday,' 'Stilpo raised his hand,' and 'Stilpo did something at noon last Tuesday' are none of them R-statements; but 'Stilpo raised his right hand at noon last Tuesday' is an R-statement.

Let us assume that it sometimes at least makes sense to speak of an agent's being able to render an R-statement true, as distinguished, for example, from simply *discovering* that it is true; and similarly, that it sometimes makes sense to speak of his being able to render an R-statement false. Thus, Stilpo could render it true that he is running at a certain time simply by running at that time, and this would be something quite different from his then merely discovering—observing, noting, etc.—that he is running. He could, of course, render the same statement false in a variety of ways—by standing still, for instance, or by lying down, and so on. We, on the other hand, could not in any similar way render *that* R-statement true. We could only discover by some means that it is true, or that it is false—by looking at Stilpo at the time in question, for instance, to *see* whether he is then running.

Further, let us assume that it sometimes at least makes sense to speak of *asking* someone to render an R-statement true. This, of course, is only an application of the general principle that, in the case of something that someone is able to do, it sometimes makes sense to ask him to do it. To illustrate, suppose that Crates has a bet with Metrocles that Stilpo will pass through the Diomean Gate at noon on the following day (call that day D). Now it surely seems to make sense that Crates might ask, and perhaps even bribe, Stilpo to do just that—to pick just that time to pass through the gate—and thus render true the R-statement 'Stilpo passes through the Diomean Gate at noon on day D.' That a request or even a bribe would not be out of place in such circumstances suggests both that it sometimes makes sense to speak of an agent's rendering an R-statement true, and that it sometimes makes sense to ask someone—namely, the agent referred to in such a statement—to do it.

Now it is easy enough to state, in general terms, what one has to do in order to render a given R-statement true. He has to do *precisely* what the statement in question says he does, at precisely the time the statement says he does it. The *only* way Stilpo can render it true that he passes through the Diomean Gate at a specific time is to pass through the gate at just that time. Similarly, the *only* way he can render it false is to refrain from passing through the gate at just that time. For someone to be *able* to render an R-statement true, then, consists simply of his being able to do something which is *logically* both necessary and sufficient for the truth of the statement to the effect that he does the thing in question at the time in question. Nothing else suffices, and this will need to be borne in mind.

Finally, we shall assume that, in case one speaks truly in uttering a particular R-statement at a particular time, then one also speaks truly in uttering the same R-statement at any other time. If, for example, one were to speak truly in saying that Stilpo is running at noon on a given Tuesday, one would also speak truly if one said the same thing again a week later, or at any other time. This, of course, is only an application of the orthodox assumption that complete statements, or the utterances of them, are not converted from true to false, or from false to true, just by the passage of time. There are some statements, to be sure, like 'Stilpo is running,' which are not, as they stand, true every time they are uttered, since it is not always the case that Stilpo is running. But that is not an R-statement. If one adds to it an explicit reference to the time at which Stilpo is alleged to be running—say, at noon on a given Tuesday—then it becomes an R-statement. It also thereby becomes a statement that is true every time it is uttered, in case it is true at all, for one can on Wednesday still say truly that Stilpo was running at noon on the day preceding, in case he was, even though Stilpo may in the meantime have stopped running. This assumption, it should be noted, does not imply that *truth* and *falsity* are 'properties' of 'propositions' that might be gained or lost through the passage of time, nor does it imply that they are not. Some say that they are, others that they are not, and still others that such a notion is meaningless to begin with; but we, at least, prefer to take no stand on that somewhat metaphysical point.

Now let us consider three times, t_1, t_2 and t_3, all of them being *past*, and t_1 being earlier than t_2 which is earlier than t_3. Consider, then, the R-statement (S):

> Stilpo walks through the Diomean Gate at t_2

and assume that statement, tenselessly expressed so as to avoid ambiguity in what follows, to be *true*. What we want to consider is: which, if any, of the following, which are not R-statements but are statements concerning Stilpo's abilities, are also true?

1. Stilpo was at t_3 able to render S false.
2. Stilpo was at t_3 able to render S true.
3. Stilpo was at t_1 able to render S false.
4. Stilpo was at t_1 able to render S true.
5. Stilpo was at t_2 able to render S false.
6. Stilpo was at t_2 able to render S true.

Now the first of these is quite evidently false. If, as assumed, it is true that Stilpo was walking through the gate at t_2, then there is absolutely nothing he (or anyone) was able to do at t_3 which could render that statement false. It was, it would seem natural to say, by that time *too late* for that. He was perhaps able at t_3 to refrain from passing through the gate again, of course, and he was perhaps able to regret that he had walked through it, to wish he had not, and so on, but his doing any of those things would not have the least tendency to render S false. Or we might think that he was at t_3 able to find conclusive evidence that he had *not* walked through the gate; but that is not in fact anything that he was able to do, for he had already walked through the gate, and hence there was at t_3 no conclusive evidence to the contrary that he could possibly find.

The second statement seems also to be clearly false. S is, we said, true. So if anyone were, at t_2 (or any other time), to assert S, he would then be speaking truly. No sense, then, can be made of Stilpo's subsequently undertaking to *render* it true. It is in this case not only too late for him to do anything about that; it is also superfluous. What he wants to do—to render S true—he has already done.

The truth or falsity of the third statement is not quite so obvious, but it certainly appears to be false, and for the same kind of reason that (1) is false. That is, if it is true that Stilpo was walking through the gate at t_2, then it is difficult to see what he (or anyone) was able to do at t_1

which might render that statement false. (Analogously to the foregoing remarks one might say, though it seems less natural to do so, that it was at that time "*too early*" for that. Stilpo was perhaps able at t_1 to refrain from then and there walking through the gate, to be sure, and perhaps he did then refrain, but that does not in the least affect the truth of S, which says nothing about what he was doing at t_1. Or we might think that he was, at t_1, able to find some conclusive evidence or indication that he was not going to walk through the gate at t_2, but that again is not anything he was able to do; for he did walk through the gate at t_2, and hence there was at t_1 no conclusive indication to the contrary that he could possibly have found.

To have been able at t_1 to render S false, Stilpo would have to have been able at t_1 to do something that would have been *logically* sufficient for the falsity of S. But nothing that he might have done at t_1 has the least logical relevance to the truth or falsity of S. We might, to be sure, suppose that he was able at t_1 firmly to resolve not to walk through the gate at t_2, but his making such a resolve would not be sufficient for the falsity of S. In fact, it has no logical relevance to S, which is, in any case, true.

Perhaps, then, Stilpo was able at t_1 to do something which would have been causally or physically sufficient for the falsity of S—to commit suicide, for example. Actually, this suggestion is irrelevant, for we have said that one renders an R-statement false only by doing something that is *logically* sufficient for its falsity. But even if it were relevant, it would not do. What is behind this suggestion is, obviously, that it is physically impossible that Stilpo should be walking through the gate at t_2 in case he killed himself at t_1. This is of course true—but if so, then it is *also* true that it was physically impossible that Stilpo should have killed himself at t_1 in case he was walking through the gate at t_2—and we have said from the start that he *was* then walking through

the gate. The only conclusion, then, is that (3) is false, even on this en-
larged and still irrelevant conception of what is involved in rendering
an R-statement false.

The fourth statement appears false for reasons similar to those given
for the falsity of (2). Namely, that S is true, or such that if anyone had
uttered S at t_1 he would then have spoken truly. No sense, then, can be
made of Stilpo's being able to do something at t_1 to *render* it true. There
would have been no point, for example, in his passing through the gate
at t_1, for that would certainly not by itself render it true that he was still
passing through the gate at t_2. Similarly, it would not have been enough
for him simply to have resolved at t_1 to pass through the gate at t_2, for
that would have been entirely compatible with the falsity of S, which
in any case neither says nor implies anything whatsoever about Stilpo's
resolutions. People do not always act upon their resolves anyway, and
there is in any case no logical necessity in their doing so. Besides, anything Stilpo might do at t_1 would be superfluous, even if it were not
pointless, for one can no more render true a statement that is true than
he can render hard a piece of clay that is hard. He can only verify that
it *is* true, and this, we have seen, is something quite different. Anything
Stilpo does at t_1, or is able to do then, is entirely wasted.

The fifth statement likewise appears to be false. If, as we are assuming, it is true that Stilpo was passing through the gate at t_2, then it is
quite impossible to see what he might be able then and there to do, in
addition to passing through the gate, which would, if done, render that
statement false. Indeed, it is logically impossible that there should be
any such supplementary action, for no matter what it was, it would have
no tendency to render S false. Even if Stilpo were to declare, most
gravely and emphatically, that he was not passing through the gate, this
would not render it false that he was—it would only render him a liar.
A condition logically sufficient for the truth of S—namely, Stilpo's
walking through the gate—already obtains at t_2, and can by no means

be conjoined with another condition logically sufficient for the falsity of that statement. Now Stilpo might, to be sure, suddenly *stop* walking through the gate, which we can for now assume that he is able to do, but this would not in the least alter the truth of S. On the contrary, unless he were walking through the gate at t_2, and unless, accordingly, S were true, he could not then *stop* walking. His ceasing to walk would only render it false that he was walking shortly after t_2; and this is hardly inconsistent with S.

The sixth statement, finally, appears, unlike the others, to be quite evidently true in one seemingly trivial sense, but nonsensical in another. The sense in which it is true is simply this: that if S is true, then it follows that Stilpo was able to be walking through the gate at t_2, that being, in fact, precisely what he was doing. It is not clear, however, what sense can be attached to his being able to render true what is true, just as it is not clear what sense could be made of someone's rendering hard some clay that is already hard.

If a piece of clay is hard we cannot sensibly ask anyone to *render* it hard. Similarly, if Stilpo is walking through the gate we cannot sensibly ask him to render it true that he is walking through the gate. We cannot sensibly ask him to *be* walking through the gate, for he is already doing that, and our request would be otiose and absurd, like asking a man who is sitting to be sitting, or one who is talking to be talking. We cannot ask him to *continue* walking through the gate, for that would not be to the point. It would, if done, only render it true that he was still walking through the gate at some time *after* t_2, which is not what we are after. And obviously, there is nothing else we could ask him to do which is anywhere to the point.

The only conclusion we can draw is that, of the six statements before us, those that make clear sense are all false, and the only one that is true makes only trivial and dubious sense. More generally, we can say that while it might, as we assumed at the beginning, make sense to speak of being able to render an R-statement true, or being able to render such a statement false, people can in fact only render true those R-statements that are true, and can only render false those that are false, and that these latter two conceptions themselves make very dubious sense.[1]

NOTES

1. I believe this paradoxical conclusion follows from the mistaken assumption that every true state has always been true. For a full-scale attack on this supposition, see my *Fate, Logic, and Time*, originally published in 1967 by Yale University Press and reprinted in 2004 by Wipf and Stock Publishers [Steven M. Cahn].

QUESTIONS

IV. LOGIC AND FREEDOM

1. If, as Ryle supposes, I guess that a horse named Eclipse will win a race, and then Eclipse does win the race, was my guess true at the time I made it?

2. Do you doubt any of Taylor's six presuppositions, do you question his reasoning, or do you accept his conclusion?

3. Do you agree with Taylor and Cahn that you cannot render true a statement that is false?

V

LOGIC AND REALITY

How are the rules of deduction to be justified? Any argument for them presumes them, and so begs the question. Susan Haack identifies two responses to this quandary: the pessimistic approach that views deduction as unjustified and the optimistic approach that views deduction as needing no justification.

How are counterfactual claims to be understood? Much of our everyday reasoning involves judgments of the form, *had p occurred, then q would have resulted*. Nelson Goodman surveys and tries to resolve the many problems that such conditionals pose.

How is the existential quantifier to be understood? For example, does the statement *Pegasus does not exist* seem to imply, paradoxically, that there is a *Pegasus*? Willard V. Quine rejects this view, arguing that "To be is to be the value of a variable."

13

The Justification of Deduction

Susan Haack

(1) It is often taken for granted by writers who propose—and, for that matter, by writers who oppose—'justifications' of *induction*, that *deduction* either does not need, or can readily be provided with, justification. The purpose of this paper is to argue that, contrary to this common opinion, problems analogous to those which, notoriously, arise in the attempt to justify induction, also arise in the attempt to justify deduction.

Hume presented us with a dilemma: we cannot justify induction deductively, because to do so would be to show that *whenever* the premisses of an inductive argument are true, the conclusion must be true too—which would be too *strong*; and we cannot justify induction inductively, either, because such a 'justification' would be *circular*. I propose another dilemma: we cannot justify deduction inductively, because to do so would be, at best, to show that *usually*, when the premisses of a deductive argument are true, the conclusion is true too—which would be *too weak*; and we cannot justify deduction deductively, either, because such a justification would be *circular*.

The parallel between the old and the new dilemmas can be illustrated thus:

Hume's dilemma
induction

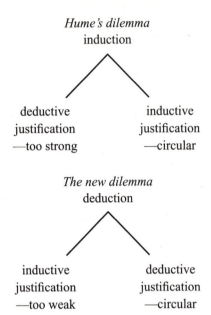

deductive   inductive
justification   justification
—too strong   —circular

The new dilemma
deduction

inductive   deductive
justification   justification
—too weak   —circular

(2) A necessary preliminary to serious discussion of the problems of justifying induction/deduction is a clear statement of them.

This means, first, giving some kind of characterisation of 'inductive argument' and 'deductive argument.' This is a more difficult task than seems to be generally appreciated. It will hardly do, for example, to characterise deductive arguments as 'non-ampliative' (Salmon [1966]) or 'explicative' (Barker [1965]), and inductive arguments as 'ampliative' or 'non-explicative'; for these characteristics are apt to turn out either false, if the key notion of 'containing nothing in the conclusion not already contained in the premises' is taken literally, or trivial, if it is not.

Because of the difficulties of demarcating 'inductive' and 'deductive' inference, it seems more profitable to define an *argument*:

An argument is a sequence $A_1 \ldots A_n$ of sentences ($n \geq I$), of which $A_1 \ldots A_{n-1}$ are the *premisses* and A_n is the *conclusion*—and then to try to distinguish inductive from deductive standards of a 'good argument.'

It is well known that deductive standards of validity may be put in either of two ways: syntactically or semantically. So:

D_1 An argument $A_1 \ldots A_{n-1} \vdash A_n$ is deductively valid (in L_D) just in case the conclusion, A_n, is deducible from the premisses, $A_1 \ldots A_{n-1}$, and the axioms of L_D, if any, in virtue of the rules of inference of L_D (the syntactic definition).

D_2 An argument $A_1 \ldots A_{n-1} \vdash A_n$ is deductively valid just in case it is impossible that the premisses, $A_1 \ldots A_{n-1}$, should be true, and the conclusion, A_n, false (the semantic definition).

Similarly, we can express standards of inductive strength either syntactically or semantically; the syntactic definition would follow D_1 but with 'L_1' for 'L_D'; the semantic definition would follow D_2 but with 'it is improbable, given that the premisses are true, that the conclusion is false.'

The question now arises, which of these kinds of characterisation should we adopt in our statement of the problems of justifying deduction/induction? This presents a difficulty. If we adopt semantic accounts of deductive validity/inductive strength, the problem of justification will seem to have been trivialised. The justification problem will reappear, however, in a disguised form, as the question '*Are there* any deductively valid/inductively strong arguments?'. If, on the other hand, we adopt syntactic accounts of deductive validity/inductive strength, the nature of the justification problem is clear: to show that arguments which are deductively valid/inductively strong are also truth-preserving/truth-preserving most of the time (i.e. deductively valid/inductively strong on the semantic accounts). On the other hand, there is the difficulty that we must somehow specify which systems are possible values of 'L$_D$' and 'L$_1$,' and this will presumably require appeal to inevitably vague considerations concerning the intentions of the authors of a formal system.

A convenient compromise is this. There are certain forms of inference, such as the rule:

R1   From: m/n of all observed F's have been G's
      to infer: m/n of all F's are G's

which are commonly taken to be inductively strong, and similarly, certain forms of inference, such as

MPP   From: $A \supset B, A$
       to infer: B

which are generally taken to be deductively valid. Analogues of the general justification problems can now be set up as follows:

> the problem of the justification of induction: show that RI is
> truth-preserving most of the time.
> the problem of the justification of deduction: show that MPP is
> truth-preserving.

My procedure will be, then, to show that difficulties arise in the attempt to justify MPP which are analogous to notorious difficulties arising in the attempt to justify RI.

(3) I consider first the suggestion that deduction *needs* no justification, that the call for a proof that MPP is truth-preserving is somehow misguided.

An argument for this position might go as follows:

> It is analytic that a deductively valid argument is truth-preserving,
> for by 'valid' we mean 'argument whose premises could not be
> true without its conclusion being true too.' So there can be no
> serious question whether a deductively valid argument is truth-
> preserving.

It seems clear enough that anyone who argued like this would be the
victim of a confusion. Agreed, if we adopt a semantic definition of 'deductively valid' it follows immediately that deductively valid arguments
are truth-preserving. But the problem was, to show that a particular form
of argument, a form deductively valid in the syntactic sense, is truth-
preserving; and *this* is a genuine problem, which has simply been
evaded. Similar arguments show the claim, made e.g. by Strawson in
[1952], p. 257, that induction needs no justification, to be confused.

(4) I argued in Section (1) that 'justifications' of deduction are liable
either to be inductive and too weak, *or* to be deductive and circular.
The former, inductive kind of justification has enjoyed little popularity
(except with the Intuitionists? cf. Brouwer [1952]). But arguments of
the second kind are not hard to find.

(*a*) Consider the following attempt to justify MPP:

A_1 Suppose that 'A' is true, and that '$A \supset B$' is true. By the truth-
table for '$\supset$,' if 'A' is true and '$A \supset B$' is true, then 'B' is true too.
So 'B' must be true too.

This argument has a serious drawback: it is of the very form which
it is supposed to justify. For it goes:

A_1' Suppose C (that 'A' is true and that '$A \supset B$' is true). If C then D (if 'A' is true and '$A \supset B$' is true, 'B' is true). So, D ('B' is true too).

The analogy with Black's 'self-supporting' argument for induction [1954] is striking. Black proposes to support induction by means of the argument:

A_2 RI has usually been successful in observed instances.
∴ RI is usually successful.

He defends himself against the charge of circularity by pointing out that this argument is not a simple case of question-begging: it does not contain its conclusion as a premiss. It might, similarly, be pointed out that A_1' is not a simple case of question-begging: for *it* does not contain its conclusion as a premiss, either.

One is inclined to feel that A_2 *is* objectionably circular, in spite of Black's defence; and this intuition can be supported by an argument, like Salmon's [1966], to show that if A_2 supports RI, an exactly analogous argument would support a counter-inductive rule, say:

RCI   From: most observed F's have not been G's
        to infer: most F's are G's.

Thus,

A_3 RCI has usually been unsuccessful in the past.
∴ RCI is usually successful.

In a similar way, one can support the intuition that there is something wrong with A_1', in spite of its not being straightforwardly question-begging, by showing that if A_1' supports MPP, an exactly analogous argument would support a deductively invalid rule, say:

MM (*modus morons*);
From: $A \supset B$ and B
to infer: A.

Thus:

A$_4$ Supposing that '$A \supset B$' is true and 'B' is true, '$A \supset B$' is true $\supset$ 'B' is true.
Now, by the truth-table for '$\supset$,' if 'A' is true, then, if '$A \supset B$' is true, 'B' is true. Therefore, 'A' is true.

This argument, like A_1, has the very form which it is supposed to justify. For it goes:

A$_4$'   Suppose D (if '$A \supset B$' is true, 'B' is true).
If C, then D (if 'A' is true, then, if '$A \supset B$' is true, 'B' is true).
So, C ('A' is true).

It is no good to protest that A_4' does not justify *modus morons* because it uses an *invalid* rule of inference, whereas A_1' does justify *modus ponens*, because it uses a *valid* rule of inference—for to justify our conviction that MPP is valid and MM is not is precisely what is at issue.

Neither is it any use to protest that A_1' is not circular because *it* is an argument in the meta-language, whereas the rule which it is supposed to justify is a rule in the object language. For the attempt to save the argument for RI by taking it as a proof, on level 2, of a rule of level 1, also falls prey to the difficulty that we could with equal justice give a counter-inductive argument, on level 2, for the counter-inductive rule at level 1. And similarly, if we may give an argument using MPP, at level 2, to support the rule MPP at level 1, we could, equally, give an argument, using MM, at level 2, to support the rule MM at level 1.

(*b*) Another way to try to justify MPP, which promises not to be vulnerable to the difficulty that, if it is acceptable, so is an analogous justification of MM, is suggested by Thomson's discussion [1963] of the Tortoise's argument. Carroll's tortoise, in [1895], refuses to draw the conclusion, '*B*,' from '$A \supset B$' and '*A*,' insisting that a new premiss, '$A \supset ((A \supset B) \supset B)$' be added; and when that premiss is granted him, will still not draw the conclusion, but insists on a further premiss, and so *ad indefinitum*. Thomson argues that Achilles should never have conceded that an extra premiss was needed; for, he argues, if the original inference was valid (semantically) the added premiss is true but not needed, and if the original inference was invalid (semantically) the added premiss is needed but false. There is an analogy, here, again, with attempts to justify induction by appending a premiss—something, usually, to the effect that 'Nature is uniform'—which turns inferences in accordance with RI into deductively valid inferences. The required premiss would, presumably, be true but not needed if RI were deductively valid, false but needed if it is not.

Thomson's idea suggests that we should contrast this picture in the case of MPP:

A_5	(1) $A \supset ((A \supset B) \supset B)$	(true but superfluous premiss)
	(2) A	assumption
	(3) $(A \supset B) \supset B$	1, 2, MPP
	(4) $A \supset B$	assumption
	(5) B	3, 4, MPP

with this picture in the case of MM:

A_6 (1) $(B \supset (A \supset B) \supset A)$ (false but needed premiss)

(2) $(A \supset B) \supset A$ assumption

(3) B 1, 2, MM

(4) $A \supset B$ assumption

(5) A 3, 4, MM

Thomson's point is that in A_5 premiss (1) is a tautology, so true; but it is not needed, since lines (2), (4) and (5) alone constitute a valid argument. In A_6, by contrast, premiss (1) is *not* a tautology; but it is needed, because lines (2), (4) and (5) alone do not constitute a valid argument. But this is to assume that MPP, which is the rule of inference in virtue of which in A_5 (2) and (4) yield (5), is valid; whereas MM, which is the rule of inference in virtue of which, in A_6, (2) and (4) would yield (5), is *not* valid. But this is just what was to have been shown.

If A_5 justifies MPP, which, after all, it uses, then the following argument equally justifies MM:

A_7 (1) $(A \supset B) \supset (A \supset B)$ (true but superfluous premiss)

(2) $A \supset B$ assumption

(3) $A \supset B$ 1, 2, MM

(4) B assumption

(5) A 3, 4, MM

In A_7 as in A_5 the first premiss is a tautology, so true, but it is superfluous, since (if MM is accepted) lines (2), (4) and (5) alone constitute a valid argument.

(*c*) Nor will it do to argue that MPP is, whereas MM is not, justified 'in virtue of the meaning of "⊃"'. For how is the meaning of '⊃' given? There are three kinds of answer commonly given: that the meaning of the connectives is given by the rules of inference/axioms of the system in which they occur; that the meaning is given by the interpretation, or, specifically, the truth-table, provided; that the meaning is given by the English readings of the connectives. Well, if '⊃' is supposed to be at least partially defined by the rules of inference governing sentences containing it (cf. Prior [1960], [1964]) then MPP and MM would be exactly on a par. In a system containing MPP the meaning of '⊃' is partially defined by the rule, from '$A \supset B$' and 'A,' to infer 'B.' In a system containing MM the meaning of '⊃' is partially defined by the rule, from '$A \supset B$' and 'B' to infer 'A.' In either case the rule in question would be justified in virtue of the meaning of '⊃,' finally, since the meaning of '⊃' would be given by the rule. If, on the other hand, we thought of '⊃' as partially defined by its truth-table (cf. Stevenson [1961]), we are in the difficulty discussed earlier ((a) above) that arguments from the truth-table to the justification of a rule of inference are liable to employ the rule in question. Nor would it do to appeal to the usual reading of '⊃' as 'if . . . then . . .,' not just because the propriety of that reading has been doubted, but also because the question, why 'B' follows from 'if A then B' and 'A' but not 'A' from 'if A then B' and 'B,' is precisely analogous to the question at issue.

(d) Our arguments against attempted justifications of MPP have appealed to the fact that analogous procedures would justify MM. So at this point it might be suggested that we can produce independent arguments against MM. (Compare attempts to diagnose incoherence in RCI.) In particular, it might be supposed that it is a relatively simple matter to show that MM cannot be truth-preserving, since with MM at our disposal we could argue as follows:

A_8 (1) $(p \& \sim p) \supset (p \vee \sim p)$
        (2) $p \vee \sim p$
        (3) $p \& \sim p$ 1, 2 MM

So that a system including MM would be inconsistent. (This idea is suggested by Belnap's paper on 'tonk.')

However, this argument is inconclusive because it depends upon certain assumptions about what else we have in the system to which MM is appended—in particular, that (1) and (2) are theorems. Now certainly *if* a system contained (1) and (2) as theorems, then (3) could be derived by MM, and the system would be inconsistent; but a system allowing MM can hardly be assumed to be otherwise conventional. (After all, many systems lack '$pv \sim p$' as a theorem; and minimal logic also lacks '$p \supset (\sim p \supset q)$'.)

(5) It might be suggested at this point that to direct our search for justification to a *form* of argument, or *argument schema*, such as MPP, is misguided, that the justification of the schema lies in the validity of its *instances*. So the answer to the question, 'What justifies the conclusion?' is simply 'The premisses'; and the answer to the further question, what justifies the argument schema, is simply that its instances are valid.

This suggestion is unsatisfactory for several reasons. First, it shifts the justification problem from the argument schema to its instances, without providing any solution to the problem of the justification of the instances, beyond the bald assertion that they *are* justified. The claim that one can just *see* that the premisses justify the conclusion is implausible in the extreme in view of the fact that people can and do disagree about which arguments are valid. Second, there is an *implicit generality* in the claim that a *particular* argument is valid. For to say that an argument is valid is not just to say that its premisses and its conclusion are true—for that is neither necessary nor sufficient for (semantic) validity. Rather, it is to say that its premisses *could not* be true without its conclusion being true also, i.e. that *there is no argument of that form with true premisses and false conclusion*. But if the claim that a particular argument is valid is to be spelled out by appeal to other arguments of that form, it is hopeless to try to justify that form of argument by appeal to the validity of its instances. (Indeed, it is not a simple matter to specify of what schema a particular argument is an instance. Our decision about what the logical form of an argument is may depend upon our view about whether the argument is valid.) Third, since a valid schema has infinitely many instances, if the validity of the schema were to be proven on the basis of the validity of its instances, the justification of the schema would have to be inductive, and would in consequence inevitably fail to establish a result of the desired strength. (Cf. Section 1.)

In rejecting this suggestion I do not, of course, deny the genetic point, that the *codification* of valid forms of inference, the *construction* of a formal system, may proceed in part via generalisation over cases— though in part, I think, the procedure may also go in the opposite direction. (This genetic point is, I think, related to the one Carnap [1968] is making when he observes that we could not convince a man who is 'deductively blind' of the validity of MPP.) But I do claim that the *justification* of a form of inference cannot derive from intuition of the validity of its instances.

(6) What I have said in this paper should, perhaps, be already familiar—it foreshadowed in Carroll [1895], and more or less explicit in Quine [1936] and Carnap 1968 ('. . . the epistemological situation in inductive logic . . . is not worse than that in deductive logic, but quite analogous to it', p. 266). But the point does not seem to have been taken.

The moral of the paper might be put, pessimistically, as that deduction is no less in need of justification than induction; or, optimistically, as that induction is in no more need of justification than deduction. But however we put it, the presumption, that induction is shaky but deduction is firm, is impugned. And this presumption is quite crucial, e.g. to Popper's proposal [1959] to replace inductivism by deductivism. Those of us who are sceptical about the analytic/synthetic distinction will, no doubt, find these consequences less unpalatable than will those who accept it. And those of us who take a tolerant attitude to nonstandard logics—who regard logic as a theory, revisable, like other theories, in the light of experience—may even find these consequences welcome.

The Problem of Counterfactual Conditionals[1]

Nelson Goodman

I. THE PROBLEM IN GENERAL

The analysis of counterfactual conditionals is no fussy little grammatical exercise. Indeed, if we lack the means for interpreting counterfactual conditionals, we can hardly claim to have any adequate philosophy of science. A satisfactory definition of scientific law, a satisfactory theory of confirmation or of disposition terms (and this includes not only predicates ending in "ible" and "able" but almost every objective predicate, such as "is red"), would solve a large part of the problem of counterfactuals. Accordingly, the lack of a solution to this problem implies that we have no adequate treatment of any of these other topics. Conversely, a solution to the problem of counterfactuals would give us the answer to critical questions about law, confirmation, and the meaning of potentiality.

I am not at all contending that the problem of counterfactuals is logically or psychologically the first of these related problems. It makes little difference where we start if we can go ahead. If the study of counterfactuals has up to now failed this pragmatic test, the alternative approaches are little better off.

What, then, is the *problem* about counterfactual conditionals? Let us confine ourselves to those in which antecedent and consequent are inalterably false—as, for example, when I say of a piece of butter that was eaten yesterday, and that had never been heated,

> If that piece of butter had been heated to 150° F., it would have melted.

Considered as truth-functional compounds, all counterfactuals are of course true, since their antecedents are false. Hence

> If that piece of butter had been heated to 150° F., it would not have melted

would also hold. Obviously something different is intended, and the problem is to define the circumstances under which a given counterfactual holds while the opposing conditional with the contradictory consequent fails to hold. And this criterion of truth must be set up in the face of the fact that a counterfactual by its nature can never be subjected to any direct empirical test by realizing its antecedent.

In one sense the name "problem of counterfactuals" is misleading, because the problem is independent of the form in which a given statement happens to be expressed. The problem of counterfactuals is equally a problem of factual conditionals, for any counterfactual can be transposed into a conditional with a true antecedent and consequent; e.g.,

> Since that butter did not melt, it wasn't heated to 150° F.

The possibility of such transformation is of no great importance except to clarify the nature of our problem. That "since" occurs in the contrapositive shows that what is in question is a certain kind of connection between the two component sentences; and the truth of this kind of statement—whether it is in the form of a counterfactual or factual conditional or some other form—depends not upon the truth or falsity of the components but upon whether the intended connection obtains. Recognizing the possibility of transformation serves mainly to focus attention on the central problem and to discourage speculation as to the nature of counterfacts. Although I shall begin my study by considering counterfactuals as such, it must be borne in mind that a general solution would explain the kind of connection involved irrespective of any assumption as to the truth or falsity of the components.

The effect of transposition upon another kind of conditional, which I call "semifactual," is worth noticing briefly. Should we assert

> Even if the match had been scratched, it still would not have lighted,

we would uncompromisingly reject as an equally good expression of our meaning the contrapositive,

> Even if the match lighted, it still wasn't scratched.

Our original intention was to affirm not that the non-lighting could be inferred from the scratching, but simply that the lighting could not be inferred from the scratching. Ordinarily a semifactual conditional has the force of denying what is affirmed by the opposite, fully counterfactual conditional. The sentence

> Even had that match been scratched, it still wouldn't have lighted

is normally meant as the direct negation of

Had the match been scratched, it would have lighted.

That is to say, in practice full counterfactuals affirm, while semifactuals deny, that a certain connection obtains between antecedent and consequent.[2] Thus it is clear why a semifactual generally has not the same meaning as its contrapositive.

There are various special kinds of counterfactuals that present special problems. An example is the ease of "counteridenticals," illustrated by the statements

> If I were Julius Caesar, I wouldn't be alive in the twentieth
> century,

and

> If Julius Caesar were I, he would be alive in the twentieth
> century.

Here, although the antecedent in the two cases is a statement of the same identity, we attach two different consequents which, on the very assumption of that identity, are incompatible. Another special class of counterfactuals is that of the "countercomparatives," with antecedents such as

> If I had more money, . . .

The trouble with these is that when we try to translate the counterfactual into a statement about a relation between two tenseless, non-modal sentences, we get as an antecedent something like

> If "I have more money than I have" were true, . . .

although use of a self-contradictory antecedent was plainly not the original intent. Again there are the "counterlegals," conditionals with antecedents that either deny general laws directly, as in

> If triangles were squares, . . .

or else make a supposition of particular fact that is not merely false but impossible, as in

> If this cube of sugar were also spherical, . . .

All these kinds of counterfactuals offer interesting but not insurmountable special difficulties.[3] In order to concentrate upon the major problems concerning counterfactuals in general, I shall usually choose my examples in such a way as to avoid these more special complications.

As I see it, there are two major problems, though they are not independent and may even be regarded as aspects of a single problem. A counterfactual is true if a certain connection obtains between the antecedent and the consequent. But as is obvious from examples already given, the consequent seldom follows from the antecedent by logic alone. (1) In the first place, the assertion that a connection holds is made on the presumption that certain circumstances not stated in the antecedent obtain. When we say

> If that match had been scratched, it would have lighted,

we mean that conditions are such—i.e., the match is well made, is dry enough, oxygen enough is present, etc.—that "That match lights" can be inferred from "That match is scratched." Thus the connection we affirm may be regarded as joining the consequent with the conjunction of the antecedent and other statements that truly describe relevant conditions. Notice especially that our assertion of the counterfactual is *not* conditioned upon these circumstances obtaining. We do not assert that the counterfactual is true *if* the circumstances obtain; rather, in asserting the counterfactual we commit ourselves to the actual truth of the statements describing the requisite relevant conditions. The first major problem is to define relevant conditions; to specify what sentences are meant to be taken in conjunction with an antecedent as a basis for inferring the consequent. (2) But even after the particular relevant conditions are specified, the connection obtaining will not ordinarily be a logical one. The principle that permits inference of

> That match lights

from

> That match is scratched. That match is dry enough. Enough oxygen is present. Etc.

is not a law of logic but what we call a natural or physical or causal law. The second major problem concerns the definition of such laws.

II. THE PROBLEM OF RELEVANT CONDITIONS

It might seem natural to propose that the consequent follows by law from the antecedent and a description of the actual state-of-affairs of the world, that we need hardly define relevant conditions because it will do no harm to include irrelevant ones. But if we say that the consequent follows by law from the antecedent and *all* true statements, we encounter an immediate difficulty:—among true sentences is the negate of the antecedent, so that from the antecedent and all true sentences everything follows. Certainly this gives us no way of distinguishing true from false counterfactuals.

We are plainly no better off if we say that the consequent must follow from *some* set of true statements conjoined with the antecedent; for given any counterfactual antecedent A, there will always be a set S—namely, the set consisting of $-A$—such that from $A \& S$ any consequent follows. (Hereafter I shall regularly use "A" for the antecedent, "C" for the consequent, and "S" for the set of statements of the relevant conditions.)

Perhaps then we must exclude statements logically incompatible with the antecedent. But this is insufficient; for a parallel difficulty arises with respect to true statements which are not logically but are otherwise incompatible with the antecedent. For example, take

If that radiator had frozen, it would have broken.

Among true sentences may well be (S)

That radiator never reached a temperature below 33° F.

Now it is certainly generally true that

All radiators that freeze but never reach below 33° F. break,

and also that

All radiators that freeze but never reach below 33° F. fail to break;

for there are no such radiators. Thus from the antecedent of the counterfactual and the given S, we can infer any consequent.

The natural proposal to remedy this difficulty is to rule that counterfactuals can not depend upon empty laws; that the connection can be established only by a principle of the form "All x's are y's" when there are some x's. But this is ineffectual. For if empty principles are excluded, the following non-empty principles may be used in the case given with the same result:

> Everything that is either a radiator that freezes but does not reach below 33° F., or that is a soap bubble, breaks;
> Everything that is either a radiator that freezes but does not reach below 33° F., or is powder, does not break.

By these principles we can infer any consequent from the A and S in question.

The only course left open to us seems to be to define relevant conditions as the set of all true statements each of which is both logically and non-logically compatible with A where non-logical incompatibility means violation of a non-logical law.[4] But another difficulty immediately appears. In a counterfactual beginning

> If Jones were in Carolina, . . .

the antecedent is entirely compatible with

> Jones is not in South Carolina

and with

> Jones is not in North Carolina

and with

> North Carolina plus South Carolina is identical with Carolina;

but all these taken together with the antecedent make a set that is self-incompatible, so that again any consequent would be forthcoming.

Clearly it will not help to require only that for *some* set *S* of true sentences, *A&S* be self-compatible and lead by law to the consequent ; for this would make a true counterfactual of

> If Jones were in Carolina, he would be in South Carolina,

and also of

> If Jones were in Carolina, he would be in North Carolina,

which can not both be true.

It seems that we must elaborate our criterion still further, to characterize a counterfactual as true if and only if there is some set *S* of true statements such that *A&S* is self-compatible and leads by law to the consequent, while there is no such set *S'* such that *A&S'* is self-compatible and leads by law to the negate of the consequent.[5] Unfortunately even this is not enough. For among true sentences will be the negate of the consequent: $\sim C$. Is $\sim C$ compatible with A or not? If not, then A alone without any additional conditions must lead by law to C. But if $\sim C$ is compatible with A (as in most cases), then if we take $\sim C$ as our S, the conjunction *A&S* will give us $\sim C$. Thus the criterion we have set up will seldom be satisfied; for since $\sim C$ will normally be compatible with A—as the need for introducing the relevant conditions testifies—there will normally be an A (namely, $\sim C$) such that *A&S* is self-compatible and leads by law to $\sim C$.

Part of our trouble lies in taking too narrow a view of our problem. We have been trying to lay down conditions under which an A that is known to be false leads to a C that is known to be false; but it is equally important to make sure that our criterion does not establish a similar connection between our A and the (true) negate of C. Because our S together with A was to be so chosen as to give us $C,$ it seemed gratuitous to specify that S must be compatible with $C;$ and because ~ C is true by supposition, S would necessarily be compatible with it. But we are testing whether our criterion not only admits the true counterfactual we are concerned with but also excludes the opposing conditional. Accordingly, our criterion must be modified by specifying that S be compatible with both C and ~ C.[6] In other words, S by itself must not decide between C and ~ C, but S together with A must lead to C but not to ~ C. We need not know whether C is true or false.

Our rule thus reads that a counterfactual is true if and only if there is some set S of true sentences such that S is compatible with C and with ~ C, and such that $A\&S$ is self-compatible and leads by law to C; while there is no set S' compatible with C and with ~ C, and such that $A\&S'$ is self-compatible and leads by law to ~ C. As thus stated, the rule involves a certain redundancy; but simplification is not in point here, for the criterion is still inadequate.

The requirement that $A\&S$ be self-compatible is not strong enough; for S might comprise true sentences that although *compatible with A*, were such that *they would not be true if A were true*. For this reason, many statements that we would regard as definitely false would be true according to the stated criterion. As an example, consider the familiar case where for a given match $M,$ we would affirm

(I)   If match M had been scratched, it would have lighted,

but deny

(II)   If match M had been scratched, it would not have been dry.[7]

According to our tentative criterion, statement II would be quite as true as statement I. For in the case of II, we may take as an element in our *S* the true sentence

Match *M* did not light,

which is presumably compatible with *A* (otherwise nothing would be required along with *A* to reach the opposite as the consequent of the true counterfactual statement, I). As our total *A&S* we may have

Match *M* is scratched. It does not light. It is well made. Oxygen enough is present . . . etc.;

and from this, by means of a legitimate general law, we can infer

It was not dry

and there would seem to be no suitable set of sentences *S'* such that *A&S'* leads by law to the negate of this consequent. Hence the unwanted counterfactual is established in accord with our rule. The trouble is caused by including in our *S* a true statement which though compatible with *A* would not be true if *A* were. Accordingly we must exclude such statements from the set of relevant conditions; *S*, in addition to satisfying the other requirements already laid down, must be not merely compatible with *A* but "jointly tenable" or "cotenable" with *A*. *A* is cotenable with *S*, and the conjunction *A&S* self-cotenable, if it is not the case that *S* would not be true if *A* were.[8]

Parenthetically it may be noted that the relative fixity of conditions is often unclear, so that the speaker or writer has to make explicit additional provisos or give subtle verbal clues as to his meaning. For

example, each of the following two counterfactuals would normally be
accepted:

> If New York City were in Georgia, then New York City would be
> in the South. If Georgia included New York City, then Georgia
> would not be entirely in the South.

Yet the antecedents are logically indistinguishable. What happens is
that the direction of expression becomes important, because in the former case the meaning is

> If New York City were in Georgia, and the boundaries of Georgia
> remained unchanged, then . . .

while in the latter case the meaning is

> If Georgia included New York City, and the boundaries of New
> York City remained unchanged, then . . .

Without some such cue to the meaning as is covertly given by the word-
order, we should be quite uncertain which of the two consequents in
question could be truly attached. The same kind of explanation accounts for the paradoxical pairs of counteridenticals mentioned earlier.

Returning now to the proposed rule, I shall neither offer further cor-
rections of detail nor discuss whether the requirement that S be cotenable with A makes superfluous some other provisions of the criterion;
for such matters become rather unimportant beside the really serious
difficulty that now confronts us. In order to determine the truth of a
given counterfactual it seems that we have to determine, among other

things, whether there is a suitable *S* that is cotenable with A and meets certain further requirements. But in order to determine whether or not a given *S* is cotenable with *A*, we have to determine whether or not the counterfactual "If *A* were true, then *S* would not be true" is itself true. But this means determining whether or not there is a suitable S_1, cotenable with *A*, that leads to ~ *S* and so on. Thus we find ourselves involved in an infinite regressus or a circle; for cotenability is defined in terms of counterfactuals, yet the meaning of counterfactuals is defined in terms of cotenability. In other words to establish any counterfactual, it seems that we first have to determine the truth of another. If so, we can never explain a counterfactual except in terms of others, so that the problem of counterfactuals must remain unsolved.

Though unwilling to accept this conclusion, I do not at present see any way of meeting the difficulty. One naturally thinks of revising the whole treatment of counterfactuals in such a way as to admit first those that depend on no conditions other than the antecedent, and then use these counterfactuals as the criteria for the cotenability of relevant conditions with antecedents of other counterfactuals, and so on. But this idea seems initially rather unpromising in view of the formidable difficulties of accounting by such a step-by-step method for even so simple a counterfactual as :

If the match had been scratched, it would have lighted.

III. THE PROBLEM OF LAW

Even more serious is the second of the problems mentioned earlier: the nature of the general statements that enable us to infer the consequent upon the basis of the antecedent and the statement of relevant conditions. The distinction between these connecting principles and relevant conditions is imprecise and arbitrary; the "connecting principles" might be conjoined to the condition-statements, and the relation of the antecedent-conjunction (*A&S*) to the consequent thus made a matter of logic. But the same problems would arise as to the kind of principle that is capable of supporting a counterfactual; and it is convenient to consider the connecting principles separately.

In order to infer the consequent of a counterfactual from the antecedent *A* and a suitable statement of relevant conditions *S*, we make use of a general statement, namely, the generalization[9] of the conditional having *A&S* for antecedent and *C* for consequent. For example, in the case of

If the match had been scratched, it would have lighted

the connecting principle is

Every match that is scratched, well made, dry enough, in enough oxygen, etc., lights.

But notice that *not* every counterfactual is actually supported by the principle thus arrived at, *even* if that principle is *true*. Suppose, for example, that all I had in my right pocket on V–E day was a group of silver coins. Now we would not under normal circumstances affirm of a given penny *P*

If P had been in my pocket on V–E day, *P* would have been silver,[10]

even though from

P was in my pocket on V–E day

we can infer the consequent by means of the general statement

Everything in my pocket on V–E day was silver.

On the contrary, we would assert that if P had been in my pocket, then this general statement would not be true. The general statement will *not* permit us to infer the given consequent from the counterfactual assumption that P was in my pocket, because the general statement will not itself withstand that counterfactual assumption. Though the supposed connecting principle is indeed general, true, and perhaps even fully confirmed by observation of all cases, it is incapable of supporting a counterfactual because it remains a description of accidental fact, not a law. The truth of a counterfactual conditional thus seems to depend on whether the general sentence required for the inference is a law or not. If so, our problem is to distinguish accurately between causal laws and casual facts.[11]

The problem illustrated by the example of the coins is closely related to that which led us earlier to require the cotenability of the antecedent and the relevant conditions, in order to avoid resting a counterfactual on any statement that would not be true if the antecedent were true. But decision as to the cotenability of two sentences must depend upon decisions as to whether or not certain general statements are laws, and we are now concerned directly with the latter problem. Is there some way of distinguishing laws from non-laws among true universal statements of the kind in question, such that a law will be the sort of principle that will support a counterfactual conditional while a non-law will not?

Any attempt to draw the distinction by reference to a notion of causative force can be dismissed at once as unscientific. And it is clear that no purely syntactical criterion can be adequate, for even the most special descriptions of particular facts can be cast in a form having any desired degree of syntactical universality. "Book *B* is small" becomes "Everything that is *Q* is small" if "*Q*" stands for some predicate that applies uniquely to *B*. What then does distinguish a law like

All butter melts at 150° F.

from a true and general non-law like

All the coins in my pocket are silver?

Primarily, I would like to suggest, the fact that the first is accepted as true while many cases of it remain to be determined, the further, unexamined cases being predicted to conform with it. The second sentence, on the contrary, is accepted as a description of contingent fact *after* the determination of all cases, no prediction of any of its instances being based upon it. This proposal raises innumerable problems, some of which I shall consider presently; but the idea behind it is just that the principle we use to decide counterfactual cases is a principle we are willing to commit ourselves to in deciding unrealized cases that are still subject to direct observation.

As a first approximation then, we might say that a law is a true sentence used for making predictions. That laws are used predictively is of course a simple truism, and I am not proposing it as a novelty. I want only to emphasize the idea that rather than a sentence being used for prediction because it is a law, it is called a law because it is used for prediction; and that rather than the law being used for prediction because it describes a causal connection, the meaning of the causal connection is to be interpreted in terms of predictively used laws.

By the determination of all instances, I mean simply the examination or testing by other means of all things that satisfy the antecedent, to decide whether all satisfy the consequent also. There are difficult questions about the meaning of "instance," many of which Professor Hempel has investigated. Most of these are avoided in our present study by the fact that we are concerned with a very narrow class of sentences: those arrived at by generalizing conditionals of a certain kind. Remaining problems about the meaning of "instance" I shall have to ignore here. As for "determination," I do not mean final discovery of truth, but only enough examination to reach a decision as to whether a given statement or its negate is to be admitted as evidence for the hypothesis in question.

The limited scope of our present problem makes it unimportant that our criterion, if applied generally to all statements, would classify as laws many statements—e.g., true singular predictions— that we would not normally call laws.

A more pertinent point is the application of the proposed criterion to vacuous generalities. As the criterion stands, no conditional with an empty antecedent-class will be a law, for all its instances will have been determined prior to its acceptance. Now since the antecedents of the statements we are concerned with will be generalizations from self-cotenable and therefore self-compatible conjunctions, none will be known to be vacuous.[12] For example, since

M is scratched. M is dry . . . (etc.)

is a self-compatible set, the antecedent of

For every x, if x is scratched and x is dry (etc.), then x lights

will not be known to be false. But now we would still want the generalized principle just given to be a law if it should just *happen* to be the case that nothing satisfies the antecedent. This discloses a defect in our criterion, which should be amended to read as follows: A true statement of the kind in question is a law if we accept it before we *know* that the instances we have determined are *all* the instances.

For convenience, I shall use the term "lawlike" for sentences which, whether they are true or not, satisfy the other requirements in the definition of law. A law is thus a sentence that is both lawlike and true, but a sentence may be true without being lawlike, as I have illustrated, or lawlike without being true, as we are always learning to our dismay.

Now the property of lawlikeness as so far defined is not only rather an accidental and subjective one but an ephemeral one that sentences may acquire and lose. As an example of the undesirable consequences of this impermanence, a true sentence that had been used predictively would cease to be a law when it became fully tested—i.e., when none of its instances remained undetermined. The definition, then, must be restated in some such way as this: A general statement is lawlike if and only if it is acceptable prior to the determination of all its instances. This is immediately objectionable because "acceptable" itself is plainly a dispositional term; but I propose to use it only tentatively, with the idea of eliminating it eventually by means of a non-dispositional definition. Before trying to accomplish that, however, we must face another difficulty in our tentative criterion of lawlikeness.

Suppose that the appropriate generalization fails to support a given counterfactual because that generalization, while true, is un-lawlike, as is

Everything in my pocket is silver.

All we would need do to get a law would be to broaden the antecedent strategically. Consider, for example, the sentence

Everything that is in my pocket or is a dime is silver.

Since we have not examined all dimes, this is a predictive statement and—since presumably true—would be a law. Now if we consider our original counterfactual and choose our S so that $A\&S$ is

P is in my pocket. P is in my pocket or is a dime,

then the pseudo-law just constructed can be used to infer from this the sentence "P is silver." Thus the untrue counterfactual is established, if one prefers to avoid an alternation as a condition-statement; the same result can be obtained by using a new predicate such as "dimo" to mean "is in my pocket or is a dime."[13]

The change called for, I think, will make the definition of law-likeness read as follows: A sentence is lawlike if its acceptance does not depend upon the determination of any given instance.[14] Naturally this does not mean that acceptance is to be independent of all determination of instances, but only that there is no particular instance on the determination of which acceptance depends. This criterion excludes from the class of laws a statement like

That book is black and oranges are spherical

on the ground that acceptance requires knowing whether the book is black; it excludes

Everything that is in my pocket or is a dime is silver

on the ground that acceptance demands examination of all things in my pocket. Moreover, it excludes a statement like

> All the marbles in this bag except Number 19 are red, and
> Number 19 is black

on the ground that acceptance would depend on examination of or knowledge gained otherwise concerning marble Number 19. In fact the principle involved in the proposed criterion is a rather powerful one and seems to exclude most of the troublesome cases.

We must still, however, replace the notion of the acceptability of a sentence, or of its acceptance *depending* or *not depending* on some given knowledge, by a positive definition of such dependence. It is clear that to say that the acceptance of a given statement depends upon a certain kind and amount of evidence is to say that given such evidence, acceptance of the statement is in accord with certain general standards for the acceptance of statements that are not fully tested. So one turns naturally to theories of induction and confirmation to learn the distinguishing factors or circumstances that determine whether or not a sentence is acceptable without complete evidence. But publications on confirmation not only have failed to make clear the distinction between confirmable and non-confirmable statements, but show little recognition that such a problem exists.[15] Yet obviously in the case of some sentences like

> Everything in my pocket is silver

or

> No twentieth-century president of the United States will be
> between 6 feet 1 inch and 6 feet 1½ inches tall,

not even the testing with positive results of all but a single instance is likely to lead us to accept the sentence and predict that the one remaining instance will conform to it; while for other sentences such as

All dimes are silver

or

All butter melts at 150° F.

or

All flowers of plants descended from this seed will be yellow

positive determination of even a few instances may lead us to accept the sentence with confidence and make predictions in accordance with it.

There is some hope that cases like these can be dealt with by a sufficiently careful and intricate elaboration of current confirmation theories; but inattention to the problem of distinguishing between confirmable and non-confirmable sentences has left most confirmation theories open to more damaging counterexamples of an elementary kind.

Suppose we designate the 26 marbles in a sack by the letters of the alphabet, using these merely as proper names having no ordinal significance. Suppose further that we are told that all the marbles except d are red, but we are not told what color d is. By the usual kind of confirmation theory this gives strong confirmation for the statement

$$Ra. Rb. Rc. Rd. \ldots Rz$$

because 25 of the 26 cases are known to be favorable while none is known to be unfavorable. But unfortunately the same argument would show that the very same evidence would equally confirm

$$Ra. Rb. Rc. Re. \ldots Rz—Rd,$$

for again we have 25 favorable and no unfavorable cases. Thus "Rd" and "$\sim Rd$" are equally and strongly confirmed by the same evidence. If I am required to use a single predicate instead of both "R" and "$\sim R$" in the second case, I will use "P" to mean:

is in the sack and either is not d and is red, or is d and is not red.

Then the evidence will be 25 positive cases for

All the marbles are P

from which it follows that d is P, which implies that d is not red. The problem of what statements are confirmable merely becomes the equivalent problem of what predicates are projectible from known to unknown cases.

So far, I have discovered no way of meeting these difficulties. Yet as we have seen, some solution is urgently wanted for our present purpose; for only where willingness to accept a statement involves predictions of instances that may be tested does acceptance endow that statement with the authority to govern counterfactual cases, which can not be directly tested.

In conclusion, then, some problems about counterfactuals depend upon the definition of cotenability, which in turn seems to depend upon the prior solution of those problems. Other problems require an adequate definition of law. The tentative criterion of law here proposed is reasonably satisfactory in excluding unwanted kinds of statements, and in effect, reduces one aspect of our problem to the question how to define the circumstances under which a statement is acceptable independently of the determination of any given instance. But this question I do not know how to answer.

NOTES

1. Slightly revised version of a paper read before the New York Philosophical Circle, May 11, 1946. My indebtedness in several matters to the work of C. I. Lewis and of C. H. Langford has seemed too obvious to call for detailed mention.

2. The practical import of a semifactual is thus different from its literal meaning. Literally a semifactual and the corresponding counterfactual are not contradictories but contraries, and both may be false (cf. footnote 8). The presence of the auxiliary terms "even" and "still," or either of them, is perhaps the idiomatic indication that a not quite literal meaning is intended.

3. Of the special kinds of counterfactuals mentioned, I shall have something to say later about counteridenticals and counterlegals. As for countercomparatives, the following procedure is appropriate:—Given "If I had arrived one minute later, I would have missed the train," first expand this to "$(\exists t)$. t is a time. I arrived (d) at t. If I had arrived one minute later than t, I would have missed the train." The counterfactual conditional constituting the final clause of this conjunction can then be treated, within the quantified whole, in the usual way. Translation into "If 'I arrive one minute later than t' were true, then 'I miss the train' would have been true" does not give us a self-contradictory component.

4. This of course raises very serious questions, which I shall come to presently, about the nature of non-logical law.

5. Note that the requirement that $A \& S$ be self-compatible can be fulfilled only if the antecedent is self-compatible; hence the conditionals I have called "counterlegal" will all be false. This is convenient for our present purpose of investigating counterfactuals that are not counterlegals. If it later appears desirable to regard all or some counterlegals as true, special provisions may be introduced.

6. It is natural to inquire whether for similar reasons we should stipulate that S must be compatible with both A and $\sim A$, but this is unnecessary. For if S is incompatible with $\sim A$, then A follows from S; therefore if S is compatible with both C and $\sim C$, then $A \& S$ can not lead by law to one but not the other. Hence no sentence incompatible with $\sim A$ can satisfy the other requirements for a suitable S.

7. Of course, some sentences similar to II, referring to other matches under special conditions, may be true; but the objection to the proposed criterion is that it would commit us to many such statements that are patently false. I am indebted to Morton G. White for a suggestion concerning the exposition of this point.

8. The double negative can not be eliminated here; for ". . . if S would be true if A were" actually constitutes a stronger requirement. As we noted earlier (footnote 2), if two conditionals having the same counterfactual antecedent are such that the consequent of one is the negate of the consequent of the other, the conditionals are contraries and both may be false. This will be the case, for example, if every otherwise suitable set of relevant conditions that in conjunction with the antecedent leads by law either to a given consequent or its negate leads also to the other.

9. The sense of "generalization" intended here is that explained by C. G. Hempel in "A Purely Syntactical Definition of Confirmation," *Journal of Symbolic Logic*, Vol. 8 (1943), pp. 122–143.

10. The antecedent in this example is intended to mean "If P, while remaining distinct from the things that were in fact in my pocket on V–E day, had also been in my pocket then," and *not* the quite different, counteridentical "If P had been identical with one of the things that were in my pocket on V–E day." While the antecedents of most counterfactuals (as, again, our familiar one about the match) are—literally speaking—open to both sorts of interpretation, ordinary usage normally calls for some explicit indication when the counteridentical meaning is intended.

11. The importance of distinguishing laws from non-laws is too often overlooked. If a clear distinction can be defined, it may serve not only the purposes explained in the present paper but also many of those for which the increasingly dubious distinction between analytic and synthetic statements is ordinarily supposed to be needed.

12. Had it been sufficient in the preceding section to require only that A&S be self-*compatible*, this requirement might now be eliminated in favor of the stipulation that the generalization of the conditional having A&S as antecedent and C as consequent should be non-vacuous; but this stipulation would not guarantee the self-*cotenability* of A&S.

13. Apart from the special class of connecting principles we are concerned with, note that under the stated criterion of lawlikeness, any statement could be expanded into a lawlike one; for example: given "This book is black" we could use the predictive sentence "This book is black and all oranges are spherical" to argue that the blackness of the book is the consequence of a law.

14. So stated, the definition counts vacuous principles as laws. If we read instead "given class of instances," vacuous principles will be non-laws since their acceptance depends upon examination of the null class of instances. For my present purposes the one formulation is as good as the other.

15. The points discussed in this and the following paragraph have been dealt with a little more fully in my "Query on Confirmation," this *Journal*, Vol. XLIII (1946), pp. 383–385.

15

On What There Is[1]

Willard V. Quine

A curious thing about the ontological problem is its simplicity. It can be put in three Anglo-Saxon monosyllables: "What is there?" It can be answered, moreover, in a word—"Everything"—and everyone will accept this answer as true. However, this is merely to say that there is what there is. There remains room for disagreement over cases; and so the issue has stayed alive down the centuries.

Suppose now that two philosophers, McX and I, differ over ontology. Suppose McX maintains there is something which I maintain there is not. McX can, quite consistently with his own point of view, describe our difference of opinion by saying that I refuse to recognize certain entities. I should protest, of course, that he is wrong in his formulation of our disagreement, for I maintain that there are no entities, of the kind which he alleges, for me to recognize; but my finding him wrong in his formulation of our disagreement is unimportant, for I am committed to considering him wrong in his ontology anyway.

When *I* try to formulate our difference of opinion, on the other hand, I seem to be in a predicament. I cannot admit that there are some things which McX countenances and I do not, for in admitting that there are such things I should be contradicting my own rejection of them.

It would appear, if this reasoning were sound, that in any ontological dispute the proponent of the negative side suffers the disadvantage of not being able to admit that his opponent disagrees with him.

This is the old Platonic riddle of non-being. Non-being must in some sense be, otherwise what is it that there is not? This tangled doctrine might be nicknamed *Plato's beard*; historically it has proved tough, frequently dulling the edge of Occam's razor.

It is some such line of thought that leads philosophers like McX to impute being where they might otherwise be quite content to recognize that there is nothing. Thus, take Pegasus. If Pegasus *were* not, McX argues, we should not be talking about anything when we use the word; therefore it would be nonsense to say even that Pegasus is not. Thinking to show thus that the denial of Pegasus cannot be coherently maintained, he concludes that Pegasus is.

McX cannot, indeed, quite persuade himself that any region of space-time, near or remote, contains a flying horse of flesh and blood. Pressed for further details on Pegasus, then, he says that Pegasus is an idea in men's minds. Here, however, a confusion begins to be apparent. We may for the sake of argument concede that there is an entity, and even a unique entity (though this is rather implausible), which is the mental Pegasus-idea; but this mental entity is not what people are talking about when they deny Pegasus.

McX never confuses the Parthenon with the Parthenon-idea. The Parthenon is physical; the Parthenon-idea is mental (according anyway to McX's version of ideas, and I have no better to offer). The Parthenon is visible; the Parthenon-idea is invisible. We cannot easily imagine two things more unlike, and less liable to confusion, than the Parthenon and the Parthenon-idea. But when we shift from the Parthenon to Pegasus, the confusion sets in—for no other reason than that McX would sooner be deceived by the crudest and most flagrant counterfeit than grant the non-being of Pegasus.

The notion that Pegasus must be, because it would otherwise be nonsense to say even that Pegasus is not, has been seen to lead McX into an elementary confusion. Subtler minds, taking the same precept as their starting point, come out with theories of Pegasus which are less patently misguided than McX's, and correspondingly more difficult to eradicate. One of these subtler minds is named, let us say, Wyman. Pegasus, Wyman maintains, has his being as an unactualized possible. When we say of Pegasus that there is no such thing, we are saying, more precisely, that Pegasus does not have the special attribute of actuality. Saying that Pegasus is not actual is on a par, logically, with saying that the Parthenon is not red; in either case we are saying something about an entity whose being is unquestioned.

Wyman, by the way, is one of those philosophers who have united in ruining the good old word "exist." Despite his espousal of unactualized possibles, he limits the word "existence" to actuality—thus preserving an illusion of ontological agreement between himself and us who repudiate the rest of his bloated universe. We have all been prone to say, in our common-sense usage of "exist," that Pegasus does not exist, meaning simply that there is no such entity at all. If Pegasus existed he would indeed be in space and time, but only because the word "Pegasus" has spatio-temporal connotations, and not because "exists" has spatio-temporal connotations. If spatio-temporal reference is lacking when we affirm the existence of the cube root of 27, this is simply because a cube root is not a spatio-temporal kind of thing, and not because we are being ambiguous in our use of "exist." However, Wyman, in an ill-conceived effort to appear agreeable, genially grants us the non-existence of Pegasus and then, contrary to what *we* meant

by non-existence of Pegasus, insists that Pegasus *is*. Existence is one
thing, he says, and subsistence is another. The only way I know of
coping with this obfuscation of issues is to *give* Wyman the word
"exist." I'll try not to use it again; I still have "is." So much for lexi-
cography; let's get back to Wyman's ontology.

Wyman's overpopulated universe is in many ways unlovely. It of-
fends the æsthetic sense of us who have a taste for desert landscapes,
but this is not the worst of it. Wyman's slum of possibles is a breeding
ground for disorderly elements. Take, for instance, the possible fat man
in that doorway; and, again, the possible bald man in that doorway. Are
they the same possible man, or two possible men? How do we decide?
How many possible men are there in that doorway? Are there more
possible thin ones than fat ones? How many of them are alike? Or
would their being alike make them one? Are no *two* possible things
alike? Is this the same as saying that it is impossible for two things to
be alike? Or, finally, is the concept of identity simply inapplicable to
unactualized possibles? But what sense can be found in talking of entities which cannot meaningfully be said to be identical with themselves
and distinct from one another? These elements are well nigh incorrigi-
ble. By a Fregean therapy of individual concepts, some effort might be
made at rehabilitation; but I feel we'd do better simply to clear
Wyman's slum and be done with it.

Possibility, along with the other modalities of necessity and impos-
sibility and contingency, raises problems upon which I do not mean to
imply that we should turn our backs. But we can at least limit modalities to whole statements. We may impose the adverb "possibly" upon
a statement as a whole, and we may well worry about the semantical
analysis of such usage; but little real advance in such analysis is to be
hoped for in expanding our universe to include so-called *possible entities*. I suspect that the main motive for this expansion is simply the

old notion that Pegasus, *e.g.*, must be because it would otherwise be nonsense to say even that he is not.

Still, all the rank luxuriance of Wyman's universe of possibles would seem to come to naught when we make a slight change in the example and speak not of Pegasus but of the round square cupola on Berkeley College. If, unless Pegasus were, it would be nonsense to say that he is not, then by the same token, unless the round square cupola on Berkeley College were, it would be nonsense to say that it is not. But, unlike Pegasus, the round square cupola on Berkeley College cannot be admitted even as an unactualized *possible*. Can we drive Wyman now to admitting also a realm of unactualizable impossibles? If so, a good many embarrassing questions could be asked about them. We might hope even to trap Wyman in contradictions, by getting him to admit that certain of these entities are at once round and square. But the wily Wyman chooses the other horn of the dilemma and concedes that it is nonsense to say that the round square cupola on Berkeley College is not. He says that the phrase "round square cupola" is meaningless.

Wyman was not the first to embrace this alternative. The doctrine of the meaninglessness of contradictions runs away back. The tradition survives, moreover, in writers such as Wittgenstein, who seem to share none of Wyman's motivations. Still I wonder whether the first temptation to such a doctrine may not have been substantially the motivation which we have observed in Wyman. Certainly the doctrine has no intrinsic appeal; and it has led its devotees to such quixotic extremes as that of challenging the method of proof by *reductio ad absurdum*—a challenge in which I seem to detect a quite striking *reductio ad absurdum eius ipsius*.

Moreover, the doctrine of meaninglessness of contradictions has the severe methodological drawback that it makes it impossible, in principle, ever to devise an effective test of what is meaningful and what is not. It would be forever impossible for us to devise systematic ways of deciding whether a string of signs made sense—even to us individually, let alone other people—or not. For it follows from a discovery in mathematical logic, due to Church, that there can be no generally applicable test of contradictoriness.

I have spoken disparagingly of Plato's beard, and hinted that it is tangled. I have dwelt at length on the inconveniences of putting up with it. It is time to think about taking steps.

Russell, in his theory of so-called singular descriptions, showed clearly how we might meaningfully use seeming names without supposing that the entities allegedly named be. The names to which Russell's theory directly applies are complex descriptive names such as "the author of *Waverly*," "the present King of France," "the round square cupola on Berkeley College." Russell analyzes such phrases systematically as fragments of the whole sentences in which they occur. The sentence, "The author of *Waverly* was a poet," *e.g.*' is explained as a whole as meaning "Someone (better: something) wrote *Waverly* and was a poet, and nothing else wrote *Waverly*." (The point of this added clause is to affirm the uniqueness which is implicit in the word "the," in "*the* author of *Waverly*.") The sentence "The round square cupola on Berkeley College is pink" is explained as "Something is round and square and is a cupola on Berkeley College and is pink, and nothing else is round and square and a cupola on Berkeley College."

The virtue of this analysis is that the seeming name, a descriptive phrase, is paraphrased *in context* as a so-called incomplete symbol. No unified expression is offered as an analysis of the descriptive phrase, but the statement as a whole which was the context of that phrase still gets its full quota of meaning—whether true or false.

The unanalyzed statement "The author of *Waverly* was a poet" contains a part, "the author of *Waverly*," which is wrongly supposed by

McX and Wyman to demand objective reference in order to be meaningful at all. But in Russell's translation, "Something wrote *Waverly*
and was a poet and nothing else wrote *Waverly*," the burden of objective
reference which had been put upon the descriptive phrase is now taken
over by words of the kind that logicians call bound variables, variables
of quantification: namely, words like "something," "nothing," "everything." These words, far from purporting to be names specifically of
the author of *Waverly*, do not purport to be names at all; they refer to
entities generally, with a kind of studied ambiguity peculiar to themselves. These quantificational words or bound variables are, of course
a basic part of language, and their meaningfulness, at least in context,
is not to be challenged. But their meaningfulness in no way presupposes
there being either the author of *Waverly* or the round square cupola on
Berkeley College or any other specifically preassigned objects.

Where descriptions are concerned, there is no longer any difficulty
in affirming or denying being. "There *is* the author of *Waverly*" is explained by Russell as meaning "Someone (or, more strictly, something)
wrote *Waverly* and nothing else wrote *Waverly*." "The author of *Waverly*
is not" is explained, correspondingly, as the alternation "Either each
thing failed to write *Waverly* or two or more things wrote *Waverly*." This
alternation is false, but meaningful; and it contains no expression purporting to designate the author of *Waverly*. The statement "The round
square cupola on Berkeley College is not" is analyzed in similar fashion.
So the old notion that statements of non-being defeat themselves goes
by the board. When a statement of being or non-being is analyzed by
Russell's theory of descriptions, it ceases to contain any expression which
even purports to name the alleged entity whose being is in question, so
that the meaningfulness of the statement no longer can be thought to
presuppose that there be such an entity. Now, what of "Pegasus"? This
being a word rather than a descriptive phrase, Russell's argument does

not immediately apply to it. However, it can easily be made to apply. We have only to rephrase "Pegasus" as a description, in any way that seems adequately to single out our idea: say, "the winged horse that was captured by Bellerophon." Substituting such a phrase for "Pegasus," we can then proceed to analyze the statement "Pegasus is," or "Pegasus is not," precisely on the analogy of Russell's analysis of "The author of *Waverly* is" and "The author of *Waverly* is not."

In order thus to subsume a one-word name or alleged name such as "Pegasus" under Russell's theory of description, we must, of course, be able first to translate the word into a description. But this is no real restriction. If the notion of Pegasus had been so obscure or so basic a one that no pat translation into a descriptive phrase had offered itself along familiar lines, we could still have availed ourselves of the following artificial and trivial-seeming device: we could have appealed to the *ex hypothesi* unanalyzable, irreducible attribute of *being Pegasus*, adopting, for its expression, the verb "is-Pegasus," or "pegasizes." The noun "Pegasus" itself could then be treated as derivative, and identified after all with a description: "the thing that is-Pegasus," "the thing that pegasizes."

If the importing of such a predicate as "pegasizes" seems to commit us to recognizing that there is a corresponding attribute, pegasizing, in Plato's heaven or in the mind of men, well and good. Neither we nor Wyman nor McX have been contending, thus far, about the being or non-being of universals, but rather about that of Pegasus. If in terms of pegasizing we can interpret the noun "Pegasus" as a description subject to Russell's theory of descriptions, then we have disposed of the old notion that Pegasus cannot be said not to be without presupposing that in some sense Pegasus is.

Our argument is now quite general. McX and Wyman supposed that we could not meaningfully affirm a statement of the form "So-and-so is not," with a simple or descriptive singular noun in place of "so-and-so," unless so-and-so be. This supposition is now seen to be quite generally groundless, since the singular noun in question can always be expanded into a singular description, trivially or otherwise, and then analyzed out *à la* Russell.

We cannot conclude, however, that man is henceforth free of all ontological commitments. We commit ourselves outright to an ontology containing numbers when we say there are prime numbers between 1000 and 1010; we commit ourselves to an ontology containing centaurs when we say there are centaurs; and we commit ourselves to an ontology containing Pegasus when we say Pegasus is. But we do not commit ourselves to an ontology containing Pegasus or the author of *Waverly* or the round square cupola on Berkeley College when we say that Pegasus or the author of *Waverly* or the cupola in question is *not*. We need no longer labour under the delusion that the meaningfulness of a statement containing a singular term presupposes an entity named by the term. A singular term need not name to be significant.

An inkling of this might have dawned on Wyman and McX even without benefit of Russell if they had only noticed—as so few of us do—that there is a gulf between *meaning* and *naming* even in the case of a singular term which is genuinely a name of an object. Frege's example will serve: the phrase "Evening Star" names a certain large physical object of spherical form, which is hurtling through space some scores of millions of miles from here. The phrase "Morning Star" names the same thing, as was probably first established by some observant Babylonian. But the two phrases cannot be regarded as having the same meaning; otherwise that Babylonian could have dispensed with his observations and contented himself with reflecting on the meanings of his words. The meanings, then, being different from one another, must be other than the named object, which is one and the same in both cases.

Confusion of meaning with naming not only made McX think he could not meaningfully repudiate Pegasus; a continuing confusion of meaning with naming no doubt helped engender his absurd notion that Pegasus is an idea, a mental entity. The structure of his confusion is as follows. He confused the alleged *named object* Pegasus with the *meaning* of the word "Pegasus," therefore concluding that Pegasus must be in order that the word have meaning. But what sorts of things are meanings? This is a moot point; however, one might quite plausibly explain meanings as ideas in the mind, supposing we can make clear sense in turn of the idea of ideas in the mind. Therefore Pegasus, initially confused with a meaning, ends up as an idea in the mind. It is the more remarkable that Wyman, subject to the same initial motivation as McX, should have avoided this particular blunder and wound up with unactualized possibles instead.

Now let us turn to the ontological problem of universals: the question whether there are such entities as attributes, relations, classes, numbers, functions. McX, characteristically enough, thinks there are. Speaking of attributes, he says: "There are red houses, red roses, red sunsets; this much is prephilosophical common-sense in which we must all agree. These houses, roses and sunsets, then, have something in common; and this which they have in common is all I mean by the attribute of redness." For McX, thus, there being attributes is even more obvious and trivial than the obvious and trivial fact of there being red houses, roses and sunsets. This, I think, is characteristic of metaphysics, or at least of that part of metaphysics called ontology: one who regards a statement on this subject as true at all must regard it as trivially true. One's ontology is basic to the conceptual scheme by which he interprets all experiences, even the most commonplace ones. Judged within some particular conceptual scheme—and how else is judgment possible?—an ontological statement goes without saying, standing in need of no separate justification at all. Ontological statements follow immediately from all manner of casual statements of commonplace fact, just as—from the point of view, anyway, of McX's conceptual scheme—"There is an attribute" follows from "There are red houses, red roses, red sunsets."

Judged in another conceptual scheme, an ontological statement which is axiomatic to McX's mind may, with equal immediacy and triviality, be adjudged false. One may admit that there are red houses, roses, and sunsets, but deny, except as a popular and misleading manner of speaking, that they have anything in common. The words "houses," "roses" and "sunsets" denote each of sundry individual entities which are houses and roses and sunsets, and the word "red" or "red object" denotes each of sundry individual entities which are red houses, red roses, red sunsets; but there is not, in addition, any entity whatever, individual or otherwise, which is named by the word "redness," nor, for that matter, by the word "househood," "rosehood," "sunsethood." That the houses and roses and sunsets are all of them red may be taken as ultimate and irreducible, and it may be held that McX is no better off, in point of real explanatory power, for all the occult entities which he posits under such names as "redness."

One means by which McX might naturally have tried to impose his ontology of universals on us was already removed before we turned to the problem of universals. McX cannot argue that predicates such as "red" or "is-red," which we all concur in using, must be regarded as names each of a single universal entity in order that they be meaningful at all. For, we have seen that, being a name of something is a much more special feature than being meaningful. He cannot even charge us—at least not by *that* argument—with having posited an attribute of pegasizing by our adoption of the predicate "pegasizes."

However, McX hits upon a different stratagem. "Let us grant," he says, "this distinction between meaning and naming of which you make so much. Let us even grant that "is red," "pegasizes," etc., are not names of attributes. Still, you admit they have meanings. But these *meanings*, whether they are *named* or not, are still universals, and I venture to say that some of them might even be the very things that I call attributes, or something to much the same purpose in the end."

For McX, this is an unusually penetrating speech; and the only way I know to counter it is by refusing to admit meanings. However, I feel no reluctance towards refusing to admit meanings, for I do not thereby deny that words and statements are meaningful. McX and I may agree to the letter in our classification of linguistic forms into the meaningful and the meaningless, even though McX construes meaningfulness as the *having* (in some sense of "having") of some abstract entity which he calls a meaning, whereas I do not. I remain free to maintain that the fact that a given linguistic utterance is meaningful (or *significant,* as I prefer to say so as not to invite hypostasis of meanings as entities) is an ultimate and irreducible matter of fact; or, I may undertake to analyze it in terms directly of what people do in the presence of the linguistic utterance in question and other utterances similar to it.

The useful ways in which people ordinarily talk or seem to talk about meanings boils down to two: the *having* of meanings, which is significance, and *sameness* of meaning, or synonomy. What is called *giving* the meaning of an utterance is simply the uttering of a synonym, couched, ordinarily, in clearer language than the original. If we are allergic to meanings as such, we can speak directly of utterances as significant or insignificant, and as synonymous or heteronymous one with another. The problem of explaining these adjectives "significant" and "synonymous" with some degree of clarity and rigor—preferably, as I see it, in terms of behaviour—is as difficult as it is important. But the explanatory value of special and irreducible intermediary entities called meanings is surely illusory.

Up to now I have argued that we can use singular terms significantly in sentences without presupposing that there be the entities which those terms purport to name. I have argued further that we can use general terms, *e.g.,* predicates, without conceding them to be names of abstract entities. I have argued further that we can view utterances as significant, and as synonymous or heteronymous with one another, without countenancing a realm of entities called meanings. At this point McX begins to wonder whether there is any limit at all to our ontological immunity. Does *nothing* we may say commit us to the assumption of universals or other entities which we may find unwelcome?

I have already suggested a negative answer to this question, in speaking of bound variables, or variables of quantification, in connection with Russell's theory of descriptions. We can very easily involve ourselves in ontological commitments by saying, *e.g.*, that *there is something* (bound variable) which red houses and sunsets have in common; or that *there is something* which is a prime number between 1000 and 1010. But this is, essentially, the *only* way we can involve ourselves in ontological commitments: by our use of bound variables. The use of alleged names is no criterion, for we can repudiate their namehood at the drop of a hat unless the assumption of a corresponding entity can be spotted in the things we affirm in terms of bound variables. Names are, in fact, altogether immaterial to the ontological issue, for I have shown, in connection with "Pegasus" and "pegasize," that names can be converted to descriptions, and Russell has shown that descriptions can be eliminated. Whatever we say with help of names can be said in a language which shuns names altogether. To be is, purely and simply, to be the value of a variable. In terms of the categories of traditional grammar, this amounts roughly to saying that to be is to be in the range of reference of a pronoun. Pronouns are the basic media of reference; nouns might better have been named pro-pronouns. The variables of quantification, "something," "nothing," "everything," range over our whole ontology, whatever it may be; and we are convicted of a particular ontological presupposition if, and only if, the alleged presuppositum has to be reckoned among the entities over which our variables range in order to render one of our affirmations true.

We may say, *e.g.*, that some dogs are white and not, thereby commit ourselves to recognizing either doghood or whiteness as entities. "Some dogs are white" says that some things that are dogs are white; and, in order that this statement be true, the things over which the bound variable "something" ranges must include some white dogs, but need not include doghood or whiteness. On the other hand, when we say that some zoological species are cross-fertile, we are committing ourselves to recognizing as entities the several species themselves, abstract though they be. We remain so committed at least until we devise some way of so paraphrasing the statement as to show that the seeming reference to species on the part of our bound variable was an avoidable manner of speaking.

If I have been seeming to minimize the degree to which in our philosophical and unphilosophical discourse we involve ourselves in ontological commitments, let me then emphasize that classical mathematics, as the example of primes between 1000 and 1010 clearly illustrates, is up to its neck in commitments to an ontology of abstract entities. Thus it is that the great mediæval controversy over universals has flared up anew in the modern philosophy of mathematics. The issue is clearer now than of old, because we now have a more explicit standard whereby to decide what ontology a given theory or form of discourse is committed to: a theory is committed to those and only those entities to which the bound variables of the theory must be capable of referring in order that the affirmations made in the theory be true.

Because this standard of ontological presupposition did not emerge clearly in the philosophical tradition, the modern philosophical mathematicians have not on the whole recognized that they were debating the same old problem of universals in a newly clarified form. But the fundamental cleavages among modern points of view on foundations of mathematics do come down pretty explicitly to disagreements as to the range of entities to which the bound variables should be permitted to refer.

The three main mediæval points of view regarding universals are designated by historians as *realism, conceptualism* and *nominalism.* Essentially these same three doctrines reappear in twentieth-century surveys of the philosophy of mathematics under the new names *logicism, intuitionism* and *formalism.*

Realism, as the word is used in connection with the mediæval controversy over universals, is the Platonic doctrine that universals or abstract entities have being independently of the mind; the mind may discover them but cannot create them. *Logicism,* represented by such latter-day Platonists as Frege, Russell, Whitehead, Church and Carnap, condones the use of bound variables to refer to abstract entities known and unknown, specifiable and unspecifiable, indiscriminately.

Conceptualism holds that there are universals but they are mind-made. *Intuitionism,* espoused in modern times in one form or another by Poincaré, Brouwer, Weyl and others, countenances the use of bound variables to refer to abstract entities only when those entities are capable of being cooked up individually from ingredients specified in advance. As Fraenkel has put it, logicism holds that classes are discovered while intuitionism holds that they are invented—a fair statement indeed of the old opposition between realism and conceptualism. This opposition is no mere quibble; it makes an essential difference in the amount of classical mathematics to which one is willing to subscribe. Logicists, or realists, are able on their assumptions to get Cantor's ascending orders of infinity; intuitionists are compelled to stop with the lowest order of infinity, and, as an indirect consequence, to abandon even some of the classical laws of real numbers. The modern controversy between logicism and intuitionism arose, in fact, from disagreements over infinity.

Formalism, associated with the name of Hilbert, echoes intuitionism in deploring the logicist's unbridled recourse to universals. But formalism also finds intuitionism unsatisfactory. This could happen for either of two opposite reasons. The formalist might, like the logicist, object to the crippling of classical mathmatics; or he might, like the *nominalists* of old, object to admitting abstract entities at all, even in the restrained sense of mind-made entities. The upshot is the same: the formalist keeps classical mathematics as a play of insignificant notations. This play of notations can still be of utility—whatever utility it has already shown itself to have as a crutch for physicists and technologists. But utility need not imply significance, in any literal linguistic sense. Nor need the marked success of mathematicians in spinning out theorems, and in finding objective bases for agreement with one another's results, imply significance. For an adequate basis for agreement among mathematicians can be found simply in the rules which govern the manipulation of the notations—these syntactical rules being, unlike the notations themselves, quite significant and intelligible.[2]

I have argued that the sort of ontology we adopt can be consequential—notably in connection with mathematics, although this is only an example. Now how are we to adjudicate among rival ontologies? Certainly the answer is not provided by the semantical formula "To be is to be the value of a variable"; this formula serves rather, conversely, in testing the conformity of a given remark or doctrine to a prior ontological standard. We look to bound variables in connection with ontology not in order to know what there is, but in order to know what a given remark or doctrine, ours or someone else's, *says* there is; and this much is quite properly a problem involving language. But what there is is another question.

In debating over what there is, there are still reasons for operating on a semantical plane. One reason is to escape from the predicament noted at the beginning of the paper: the predicament of my not being able to admit that there are things which McX countenances and I do not. So long as I adhere to my ontology, as opposed to McX's, I cannot allow my bound variables to refer to entities which belong to McX's ontology and not to mine. I can, however, consistently describe our disagreement by characterizing the statements which McX affirms. Provided merely that my ontology countenances linguistic forms, or at least concrete inscriptions and utterances, I can talk about McX's sentences.

Another reason for withdrawing to a semantical plane is to find common ground on which to argue. Disagreement in ontology involves basic disagreement in conceptual schemes; yet McX and I, despite these basic disagreements, find that our conceptual schemes converge sufficiently in their intermediate and upper ramifications to enable us to communicate successfully on such topics as politics, weather and, in particular, language. In so far as our basic controversy over ontology can be translated upward into a semantical controversy about words and what to do with them, the collapse of the controversy into question-begging may be delayed.

It is no wonder, then, that ontological controversy should tend into controversy over language. But we must not jump to the conclusion that what there is depends on words. Translatability of a question into semantical terms is no indication that the question is linguistic. To see Naples is to bear a name which, when prefixed to the words "see Naples," yields a true sentence; still there is nothing linguistic about seeing Naples.

Our acceptance of an ontology is, I think, similar in principle to our acceptance of a scientific theory, say, a system of physics: we adopt, at least insofar as we are reasonable, the simplest conceptual scheme into which the disordered fragments of raw experience can be fitted and arranged. Our ontology is determined once we have fixed upon the overall conceptual scheme which is to accommodate science in the broadest sense; and the considerations which determine a reasonable construction of any part of that conceptual scheme, *e.g.*, the biological or the physical part, are not different in kind from the considerations which determine a reasonable construction of the whole. To whatever extent the adoption of any system of scientific theory may be said to be a matter of language, the same—but no more—may be said of the adoption of an ontology.

But simplicity, as a guiding principle in constructing conceptual schemes, is not a clear and unambiguous idea; and it is quite capable of presenting a double or multiple standard. Imagine, *e.g.*, that we have devised the most economical set of concepts adequate to the play-by-play reporting of immediate experience. The entities under this scheme—the values of bound variables—are, let us suppose, individual subjective events of sensation or reflection. We should still find, no doubt, that a physicalistic conceptual scheme, purporting to talk about external objects, offers great advantages in simplifying our overall reports. By bringing together scattered sense events and treating them as perceptions of one object, we reduce the complexity of our stream of experience to a manageable conceptual simplicity. The rule of simplicity is indeed our guiding maxim in assigning sense data to objects: we associate an earlier and a later round sensum with the same so-called penny, or with two different so-called pennies, in obedience to the demands of maximum simplicity in our total world-picture.

Here we have two competing conceptual schemes, a phenomenalistic one and a physicalistic one. Which should prevail? Each has its advantages; each has its special simplicity in its own way. Each, I suggest, deserves to be developed. Each may be said, indeed, to be the more fundamental, though in different senses: the one is epistemologically, the other physically, fundamental.

The physical conceptual scheme simplifies our account of experience because of the way myriad scattered sense events come to be associated with single so-called objects; still there is no likelihood that each sentence about physical objects can actually be translated, however deviously and complexly, into the phenomenalistic language. Physical objects are postulated entities which round out and simplify our account of the flux of experience, just as the introduction of irrational numbers simplifies laws of arithmetic. From the point of view of the conceptual scheme of the elementary arithmetic of rational numbers alone, the broader arithmetic of rational and irrational numbers would have the status of a convenient myth, simpler than the literal truth (namely, the arithmetic of rationals) and yet containing that literal truth as a scattered part. Similarly, from a phenomenalistic point of view, the conceptual scheme of physical objects is a convenient myth, simpler than the literal truth and yet containing that literal truth as a scattered part.

Now what of classes or attributes of physical objects, in turn? A platonistic ontology of this sort is, from the point of view of a strictly physicalistic conceptual scheme, as much of a myth as that physicalistic conceptual scheme itself was for phenomenalism. This higher myth is a good and useful one, in turn, in so far as it simplifies our account of physics. Since mathematics is an integral part of this higher myth, the utility of this myth for physical science is evident enough. In speaking of it nevertheless as a myth, I echo that philosophy of mathematics to which I alluded earlier under the name of formalism. But my present suggestion is that an attitude of formalism may with equal justice be adopted toward the physical conceptual scheme, in turn, by the pure aesthete or phenomenalist.

The analogy between the myth of mathematics and the myth of physics is, in some additional and, perhaps, fortuitous ways, strikingly close. Consider, for example, the crisis which was precipitated in the foundations of mathematics, at the turn of the century, by the discovery of Russell's paradox and other antinomies of set theory. These contradictions had to be obviated by unintuitive, *ad hoc* devices; our mathematical myth-making became deliberate and evident to all. But what of physics? An antinomy arose between the undular and the corpuscular accounts of light; and if this was not as out-and-out a contradiction as Russell's paradox, I suspect that the reason is merely that physics is not as out-and-out as mathematics. Again, the second great modern crisis in the foundations of mathematics—precipitated in 1931 by Godel's proof that there are bound to be undecidable statements in arithmetic—has its companion-piece in physics in Heisenberg's indeterminacy principle.

In earlier pages I undertook to show that some common arguments in favour of certain ontologies are fallacious. Further, I advanced an explicit standard whereby to decide what the ontological commitments of a theory are. But the question what ontology actually to adopt still stands open, and the obvious counsel is tolerance and an experimental spirit. Let us by all means see how much of the physicalistic conceptual scheme can be reduced to a phenomenalistic one; still, physics also naturally demands pursuing, irreducible *in toto* though it be. Let us see how, or to what degree, natural science may be rendered independent of platonistic mathematics; but let us also pursue mathematics and delve into its platonistic foundations.

From among the various conceptual schemes best suited to these various pursuits, one—the phenomenalistic—claims epistemological priority. Viewed from within the phenomenalistic conceptual scheme, the ontologies of physical objects and mathematical objects are myths.

The quality of myth, however, is relative; relative, in this case, to the epistemological point of view. This point of view is one among various, corresponding to one among our various interests and purposes.

NOTES

1. This is a revised version of a paper which was presented before the Graduate Philosophy Club of Yale University on May 7, 1948. The latter paper, in turn, was a revised version of one which was presented before the Graduate Philosophical Seminary of Princeton University on March 15, 1951.

2. See Goodman and Quine, "Steps toward a constructive nominalism" *Journal of Symbolic Logic,* vol. 12 (1947), pp. 97–122.

QUESTIONS

V. LOGIC AND REALITY

1. Provide an example of a counterfactual and indicate how its truth would be determined.

2. Why do we believe the laws of logic?

3. What does Quine mean by his claim that "to be is to be the value of a variable"?

ABOUT THE CONTRIBUTORS

1. Lewis Carroll was the pseudonym of Charles Lutwidge Dodgson, who taught mathematics at Oxford University and wrote the immortal children's books *Alice's Adventures in Wonderland* (1865) and its sequel *Through the Looking-Glass and What Alice Found There* (1872).

2. W. J. Rees was a Senior Lecturer at Leeds University.

3. J. F. Thomson was Professor of Philosophy at M.I.T.

4. A. N. Prior was a Fellow at Balliol College, Oxford University.

5. J. T. Stevenson is Emeritus Professor of Philosophy at the University of Toronto.

6. Nuel D. Belnap is Professor of Philosophy at the University of Pittsburgh.

7. Vann McGee is Professor of Philosophy at M.I.T.

8. E. J. Lowe is Professor of Philosophy at Durham University.

9. D. E. Over teaches at the School of Humanities and Social Sciences at University of Sunderland.

10. Gilbert Ryle was Waynflete Professor of Metaphysical Philosophy at Oxford University.

11. Richard Taylor was Professor of Philosophy at the University of Rochester.

12. Steven M. Cahn, co-editor of this book, is Professor of Philosophy at the City University of New York Graduate Center.

13. Susan Haack is Professor of Law and Philosophy at the University of Miami.

14. Nelson Goodman was Professor of Philosophy at Harvard University.

15. Willard V. Quine was Professor of Philosophy at Harvard University.

SOURCE CREDITS

Lewis Carroll, "What the Tortoise said to Achilles," *Mind* 4 (1895): 278–280.

W. J. Rees, "What Achilles Said to the Tortoise," *Mind* 60 (1951): 241–246.

J. F. Thomson, "What Achilles Should have Said to the Tortoise," *Ratio* 3 (1960): 95–105.

A. N. Prior, "The Runabout Inference Ticket," *Analysis* 21 (1960): 38–39.

J. T. Stevenson, "Roundabout the Runabout Inference Ticket," *Analysis* 21 (1961): 124–128.

Nuel D. Belnap, "Tonk, Plonk, and Plink," *Analysis* 22 (1962): 130–134.

Vann McGee, "A Counterexample to Modus Ponens," *Journal of Philosophy* 82 (1985): 462–471.

E. J. Lowe, "Not A Counterexample to Modus Ponens," *Analysis* 47 (1987): 44–47.

D. E. Over, "Assumptions and the Supposed Counterexamples to Modus Ponens," *Analysis* 47 (1987) 142–146.

Gilbert Ryle, "It Was to Be," from Gilbert Ryle, *Dilemmas* (Cambridge University Press, 1954), pp. 15–35.

Richard Taylor, "Fatalism," *The Philosophical Review* 71 (1962): 56–66.

Steven M. Cahn and Richard Taylor, "Time, Truth, and Ability," *Analysis* 25 (1964): 137–141.

Susan Haack, "The Justification of Deduction," *Mind* 85 (1976): 112–119.

Nelson Goodman, "The Problem of Counterfactual Conditionals," *Journal of Philosophy* 44 (1947): 113–120.

Willard V. Quine, "On What There Is," *Review of Metaphysics* 2 (1948): 21–38.